First aid

Here are some hints to help you if your exams are coming up quickly and you don't have time to read the whole book. Look for the bandaids!

If your exams are in one to two weeks...

To start with, you will need to calm down your body and mind. Calming either one of these aspects will help calm the other.

Bandaids to calm your body:

Bandaid 1   Teach yourself the centering breath. Instructions are on page 42 and on track 2 of the CD (other uses of this technique are on pages 78 to 80 and 99).

Bandaid 2   Do some exercise (see page 80).

Bandaid 3   Sleep well. Read the hints on pages 82 to 83 and listen to track 4 on the CD.

Bandaids to calm your mind:

Bandaid 4   Challenge stressful thoughts. Examples and instructions on how to do this are on pages 113 to 114.

Bandaid 5   Think about positive memories or fantasies. Ideas on how to do this are on pages 125, 128 and 129.

Bandaids to use once you have calmed down:

Bandaid 6   Ask for any help or support you need. You will find advice on doing this on pages 88 to 89.

Bandaid 7   Organise yourself well in the time you have left. Read the pages on goal setting on pages 93 to 99.

Bandaid 8   Learn in active ways that help your concentration and memory. Tips on how to do this are on pages 103 to 105.

Bandaid 9   Find out as much information about the exam as possible, as suggested on pages 92 and 105 to 106.

Bandaid 10   If you are a perfectionist, read about how you can combat perfectionism on pages 150 to 151.

Bandaid 11   If you are a procrastinator, read about ways to combat procrastination on page 165.

Bandaid 12   Listen to the positive visualisation on track 3 on the CD as often as you can. More information about this track is on pages 129 to 131.

Bandaid 13   Read chapter 15 to find out what to do in the evening before an exam, in the morning before an afternoon exam and when you are actually in the exam room.

Bandaid 14   Use your institution's counselling service if necessary.

If your exams are in one to two days...

Calm your body and mind (bandaids 1, 4 and 5) and get a good night's sleep (bandaid 3).

Get some support, particularly emotionally (bandaids 6 and 14).

Listen to track 3 on the CD twice a day (bandaid 12).

Read the sections in part VI about what to do immediately before and during an exam (bandaid 13).

Remember to read the entire book once your exams are over. Promise yourself now that you will do this.

EXAM STRESS?

NO WORRIES!

Su Dorland

Wrightbooks

First published 2009 by Wrightbooks
an imprint of John Wiley & Sons Australia, Ltd
42 McDougall Street, Milton Qld 4064

Office also in Melbourne

Typeset in Berkeley LT 11.5/14.5pt

© Su Dorland 2009

The moral rights of the author have been asserted

National Library of Australia Cataloguing-in-Publication data:

Author:	Dorland, Su.
Title:	Exam stress? No worries! / Su Dorland.
ISBN:	9781742169583 (pbk.)
Notes:	Includes index. Bibliography.
Subjects:	Test anxiety. Test anxiety — Prevention. Test-taking skills. Stress management.
Dewey Number:	371.26019

Printed in China by Printplus Limited

CD recording by Brett Van Hoorn, Van Hoorn Music. Warning: listening to the accompanying CD may cause drowsiness or reduced awareness. While listening, avoid tasks that require alertness.

10 9 8 7 6 5 4 3 2 1

Disclaimer

The material in this publication is of the nature of general comment only, and does not represent professional advice. It is not intended to provide specific guidance for particular circumstances and it should not be relied on as the basis for any decision to take action or not take action on any matter which it covers. Readers should obtain professional advice where appropriate, before making any such decision. To the maximum extent permitted by law, the author and publisher disclaim all responsibility and liability to any person, arising directly or indirectly from any person taking or not taking action based upon the information in this publication.

Contents

About the author

Su Dorland has been a full-time, part-time, off-campus and mature-age student in both England and Australia. She started her career as a sociologist, teaching in schools, colleges and universities. Since deciding to retrain as a psychologist and counsellor, she has spent more than 30 years working as a counsellor in tertiary settings. One of her specialities is helping students deal with their exam anxiety.

Su is a Fellow of the Australia and New Zealand Student Services Association and a member of the Australian Psychological Society and its College of Counselling Psychologists. In addition, she is a certified Clinical Transactional Analyst (TA) and has also trained in other therapeutic modalities. She has continually refined her ideas, based on transactional analysis and cognitive behaviour therapy, into a package that works for students.

Su lives with her husband, John Davies, on the idyllic far-north coast of New South Wales, where she works part-time in a private practice and writes.

Acknowledgements

This book is the product of many years spent working as a counsellor in educational settings and is based on my training in various therapeutic modalities, including transactional analysis (TA). I have adapted relevant parts of TA theory with the view to making the book easily understood. I acknowledge that TA is an extremely complex theory of personal change and that the book doesn't reflect this complexity. It was not meant to.

Thanks to the students, colleagues and professional friends that commented on various drafts of this book. These people include Anna Weatherly (whose valuable professional input has been available to me throughout the whole process), Anne Gates, Rosie McKellar, Margaret Stimpson, Kirsty Taylor, Brigid Ballard and Lilian Wissink. Thanks also to Sue Burton for her comments on the CD scripts and to Eileen Corrigan for some technical assistance.

Mary Masters from John Wiley & Sons recognised the book's potential from a publisher's perspective, and Jana Adzic's remarkable editing skills have been invaluable in polishing the final text. The Wiley team's insight and high level of professional competence as they steered the book, and me, through the publishing process has been a rewarding experience in itself.

The writing process, from first idea to publishing, took more time than I originally expected due to unforseen circumstances. My husband, John Davies, gave me his total support and encouragement and helped me keep going until the end. I give him a very special thank you.

Preface
Is this book for you?

Worry a little bit every day and in a lifetime you will lose a couple of years. If something is wrong, fix it if you can. But train yourself not to worry. Worry never fixes anything.

— Mary Hemingway (1908–1986)

Do you:

⇨ feel stressed, nervous, anxious, or even terrified before or during a written or oral exam?

⇨ provide support to a friend, relative, student or client who fits the description above?

If so, this book and its accompanying CD are for you.

There is no need to be stressed out about exams. It is possible to get rid of your exam anxiety forever. And the skills you will learn from this book will also transfer to other aspects of your life, such as job interviews, driving tests, public speaking, or any other situation where high stress levels can get in the way of you doing your personal best.

I have written this book for students who get stressed about their exams, their support people (who could be counsellors, teachers, therapists, friends or relatives), and for those who are simply curious as to why people get so stressed out over exams. For simplicity's sake, I have addressed the book to students, but anyone can read it. You can work through it alone, or you may like to do so with someone else, such as a friend or counsellor.

This book is relevant for students in their final year at school, college students, university students, or students doing short courses that involve exams. It is also suitable for prospective students. Basically, whatever type of student you are and whatever type of course you are doing, if you get stressed about exams this is the book for you.

When you are stressed, nervous, anxious, or even terrified about exams do you:

⇨ put off your revision?

⇨ not plan your revision, or not stick to your plan?

⇨ not take in what you are revising?

⇨ get easily distracted?

⇨ feel tired during the day for no apparent reason?

⇨ find it difficult to sleep as the exam approaches?

⇨ go 'blank' in the exam room or dread doing so?

⇨ become unable to speak or think clearly in an oral exam?

⇨ find yourself working out how you can best claim a handicap to get some sort of special consideration or postpone the exam?

⇨ desperately want to avoid failure because you would find it so hard to admit that you failed?

⇨ tell yourself that life won't be worth living if you don't pass?

⇨ tell yourself you are not going to pass, or not pass well enough?

⇨ worry that you will let someone down if you fail?

⇨ get an upset stomach, or other physical problems, as the exam approaches?

⇨ think about past exam failures?

⇨ want to drop out of your course?

If any of the above sounds familiar, then this book and accompanying CD can help you change your thinking, feelings and behaviour.

In the weeks before an exam you may also have found yourself doing one or more of the following:

⇨ arguing more often with your partner, parents, friends, children or colleagues

⇨ feeling more emotional than usual—for example, crying more easily

⇨ constantly checking things that the rational side of you knows there is no need to check—for example, that the front door is locked

⇨ eating less or more than usual

⇨ drinking more alcohol or taking other drugs, including over-the-counter medication

⇨ starting to develop odd habits, such as scratching yourself

⇨ breaking up with your girlfriend, boyfriend or partner

⇨ having accidents you could have avoided

⇨ spending more time on the internet or writing unimportant emails

⇨ cleaning your room or house more often.

All sorts of feelings and events start crawling out of the woodwork around exam time. As exams draw closer, some students start to experience more problems than usual. On the surface, these problems may not seem directly related to exams; however, as we get more anxious, our thoughts, feelings and behaviour can change quite dramatically, and other aspects of our lives can be badly affected. When we are anxious we can miss making the connection between our anxiety and the fact that we are facing difficult problems in our lives. We can even find ourselves in difficult personal situations around exam time and not even realise we are anxious about our exams! Knowing that it doesn't have to be like this is what inspired me to write this book.

How anxious do you get about exams?

Rate yourself on the following scale before you read any further. You will need to rate yourself again once you have worked through the book and completed at least one exam, so that you can monitor your improvement. You will have a chance to do this in chapter 15.

In the following table circle the number that best corresponds to your anxiety when your exams are close, and when you're actually taking an exam.

My anxiety level	When exams are close	During an exam
I have no anxiety	0	0
I am slightly anxious	1	1

My anxiety level	When exams are close	During an exam
I am fairly anxious	2	2
I am very anxious	3	3
I am extremely anxious	4	4
I am in a total panic	5	5

Research into exam anxiety consistently shows that a large number of students suffer from exam anxiety, whether they are at school, college or university. In other words, being anxious about exams is a common problem. It has also been shown that suffering from exam anxiety can significantly lower your results. Do you think that your anxiety affects your exam results? Rate your answer in the following table.

I don't know if my anxiety affects my results	0
My anxiety affects my results a little	1
My anxiety affects my results quite a bit	2
My anxiety affects my exam results considerably	3

In need of a quick fix?

There is no magic wand to make your anxiety disappear completely, but I know that many of you picking up this book are looking for a 'quick fix' because your exams are close. The first aid hints at the front of this book provide some emergency help for those who need it and who haven't got time to read the whole book. These tips will probably not cure you of your exam anxiety, but may help you to get through your exams in the short term if they are very close. The first aid hints refer you to relevant pages in the book where you will see a bandaid splashed across the page.

These tips are more like bandaids than a cure.

Prefer a permanent cure?

If you want your exam anxiety to go away for good I recommend that you take a closer look at this book once the pressure of exams has lifted. You will need to take a longer-term approach and work your way through the book in its entirety for a permanent cure. This will help you understand why you get anxious and address the cause of your anxiety. You will need to read, complete the exercises and listen to the CD, and do so when you are not in a panic about exams—perhaps when you're on holidays or during semester break. Remember that exam anxiety will only disappear completely if you address what's causing it. Give yourself time to do this and you will get rid of your exam stress once and for all.

Twenty-first-century students – a mixed bunch

As a student you might be at school, college or university. These days, as well as studying at different types of institutions, students are a mixed bunch in other ways. For example, you might be:

⇨ a full-time student who works part-time

⇨ a part-time student who may or may not be working full-time

⇨ a student studying through the off-campus mode

⇨ a mature-aged student (aged 21 and over)

⇨ an Australian student where English is not your first language or not normally spoken at home

⇨ an international student who intends to go home after completing your course

⇨ a combination of some of the above.

All students are under a certain amount of pressure that differs depending on the type of student they are. These pressures may be external (from parents, school, friends and so on) and add to the internal pressures we put on ourselves. Some examples of external pressure are financial problems, lack of time, exams that are worth 100 per cent of assessment, or the pressure to get a high mark to get a particular job. This book in no way discounts the very real pressures that come from the outside. You may have taken time out of paid employment to get your qualification, or you may need to get a reasonable mark in order to continue with further study. Luckily, you can learn ways to avoid letting these pressures get on top of you.

This is not another study skills book

There are plenty of study skills books around, but this is *not* one of them. Rather, it is about the external and internal pressures students face with regards to exams, and, more importantly, what students can do about them. This book concentrates only on the study skills that are designed to prevent exam anxiety—it won't teach you how to write essays or read more efficiently. (If you do want to improve these types of skills, refer to the list of books on study skills in the further reading section at the end of the book.)

How to use the accompanying CD

Track 1 is an introduction by me.

Track 2 contains instructions on how to calm down on the spot. This technique is often referred to as 'centering' and is useful for any occasion where you may feel uptight, such as just before you sit down to study, just before an exam or just before an oral presentation of some sort. This technique is also transferable to other situations where you could feel nervous, such as going to a job interview or walking in to a room full of strangers.

Track 3 is to be used on a regular basis in the lead-up to your exam. It contains a relaxation sequence followed by an imaginary journey (often called a visualisation) of you successfully taking the exam. When you can listen to this track and remain positive, relaxed and focused throughout your imaginary journey, you should feel the same way when actually taking an exam.

Track 4 will help you get a good night's sleep and should be put on when you are ready to go to bed. It is the last track on the CD so that you can listen and fall asleep as it plays without being woken by a following track.

Warning: listening to this CD may cause drowsiness or reduced awareness. While listening, avoid tasks that require alertness.

A word of warning

Some chapters, particularly chapter 2, contain pencil and paper exercises for you to complete in a notebook. You must keep your notebook handy and take your time to do these because it is only by completing them thoughtfully and honestly that they will work for you. No-one needs to see your answers—they are not exams!

Some exercises ask you to search quite deeply into particular parts of your life, and you could find this quite uncomfortable or confronting. It is not my intention to make you feel this way, but if you do you will probably have found the reason for your exam anxiety. This is a positive thing because you can then go on to do something about it! On the other hand, if you feel threatened by any of the exercises I suggest you stop and get help to deal with your feelings. Talk to an understanding friend, a relative or a counsellor. Most educational institutions have counsellors you can talk to about what you're going through, and they can also point you in the direction of any other local resources.

Journeys of self-discovery can be exciting, fun and, at times, challenging. By the end of your journey with me I hope that you will come to see that exams are not the huge obstacle or monster you previously thought them to be.

Keep in mind one of my favourite quotes, by Joseph Goldstein: 'You can't stop the waves but you can learn to surf'.

Let's get started!

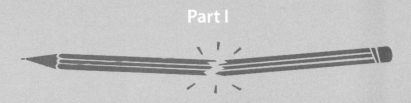

Why do some people get anxious and not others?

A crust eaten in peace is better than a banquet partaken in anxiety.

—Aesop (620BC–560BC)

Part I of this book has two chapters. Chapter 1 will give you enough information about anxiety to help you understand why exams can make students anxious. Chapter 2 explains why we react to exams in different ways. In chapter 2 you will be introduced to some ideas that students have found to be particularly useful in helping to change their attitude towards exams. There are also plenty of case studies to help you understand the ideas.

For students to be successful they usually have to pass exams, and many find the big 'e' word scary, if not terrifying. This part of the book explores why some of us turn exams into our own personal monsters, while others seem to sail through and even enjoy them.

Part I of this book will explain why these different reactions to exams occur.

Chapter 1

Why exams can make students anxious

As we all know, not everyone experiences exams in the same way. Some students get stressed out and anxious thinking about exams, in the lead-up to or during an exam, or at all of these times.

Anxiety can take many forms. Some students feel worried, get tense, feel panicky, have a huge sense of unease, feel sheer terror, or have any combination of these horrible feelings at varying levels of intensity.

Exams are usually unavoidable and compulsory, and can be viewed by exam-anxious students as huge monsters. There is generally no way of getting out of an exam, although some exam-anxious people may fantasise about doing so! In addition, exam-anxious students usually end up getting lower marks than they would have if they were not so anxious, because their anxiety has gotten in the way of thinking and remembering clearly.

What is anxiety?

To understand anxiety it is first necessary to explain the difference between anxiety and fright. Fright is a response to a *realistic* threatening situation, such as being attacked by a dog or being caught in an ocean rip. Anxiety is a response to an *unrealistic* threatening situation, such as seeing a mouse in your garden or revising for upcoming exams.

When we get frightened or anxious things start to happen both outside and inside of our bodies to help us cope with the situation. This reaction is often referred to as the alarm reaction or the fight-or-flight response. The alarm reaction automatically occurs when we are either frightened or anxious. It is a useful reaction because it prepares our bodies to deal with the perceived threat so that we can either fight it or run away from it.

You can get a fairly good sense of the alarm reaction by pretending to be suddenly surprised or startled by a threatening situation. Try doing this now. Pretend that you are an actor on stage and have to play a character that is suddenly surprised by something. Hold the position for as long as you can and, at the same time, take note of what your body is doing. More than likely you will:

⇨ suck in air and stop breathing

⇨ pull up your shoulders

⇨ be up on your toes with stiff legs.

In other words, you are 'up and tight', which is where the word 'uptight' comes from.

If you were not pretending, your body would be preparing itself to act on the inside, too. For example:

⇨ your heart rate and blood pressure would increase

⇨ your liver would release extra sugar to fuel your muscles

⇨ your digestion would slow down (because your body needs all the energy it can get to deal with the threat).

When the threat is over your body will return to its normal equilibrium. After a fright you may experience feeling wobbly, needing to sit down, needing to take long breaths and perhaps crying to let out some of the tension you experienced.

The problem with these responses is that our bodies can't tell the difference between being frightened and being anxious. The alarm reaction kicks in automatically if we think we are faced with a threat, whether it is realistic (when we respond with fear) or unrealistic (when we respond with anxiety). The alarm reaction can continue for many weeks if we are anxious about a situation that won't go away, such as exams, or if we are anxious about several different situations. Over time, this tension in our bodies can turn into chronic anxiety and even become visible.

For example, if you are chronically anxious, you may have the following symptoms:

⇨ your brows are pulled together and you get a crease at the top of your nose

⇨ the muscles of your eyes and forehead are tight

⇨ your eyes are wide open and the pupils dilated

⇨ there is a worried look on your face

⇨ your lips are pursed

⇨ your jaw is tense

⇨ your breathing is shallow.

On the inside of your body, other changes can occur if you are chronically anxious:

⇨ your larynx tightens, which affects the way you speak and breathe

⇨ your tongue is coated and your mouth gets dry

⇨ your blood vessels constrict and your heart rate increases

⇨ your blood pressure rises

⇨ your muscles become chronically tense

⇨ your blood sugar level is upset

⇨ air starts collecting in your stomach so it feels distended

⇨ you start grinding your teeth at night

⇨ you get headaches and other bodily aches and pains.

It is important to note that although these symptoms could be signs of being uptight, there could be other medical reasons for them, too. It is always wise to consult your doctor if you are suffering from any of these symptoms.

As exams can take place regularly over several years, if you are anxious about them, the threat stays with you. You could begin to look and feel anxious for the long term, and eventually become sick.

How much anxiety is too much?

You may tell yourself 'Everyone feels some anxiety around exam time. It's normal'. This is true to an extent. A student who is not anxious about exams will probably still feel some level of stimulation or anticipation when an exam is approaching, reflecting a low level of pressure. They may feel 'keyed up' and can use this positive energy to their advantage.

On the other hand, an exam-anxious student will experience a high level of pressure, which is technically referred to as 'arousal'. When a student feels a high level of pressure he or she is experiencing the alarm reaction, which will affect him or her physically and psychologically. We all need some low-level pressure before an event such as an exam to perform well, but low-level pressure does not cause anxiety—it helps us achieve our personal best. However, if we experience too much pressure, we become anxious and don't perform as well.

Figure 1.1 (overleaf) illustrates the relationship between pressure, anxiety and performance. It shows that we need some pressure to do our personal best in any exciting or challenging situation, but if we experience too much then anxiety takes over and our performance level drops off.

For this reason, I will not be helping you to become so relaxed that you don't have the energy to revise and write your exam at your best level of ability. I want to help you sit your exam with enough pressure to put you at the top of the curve so that you perform at your personal best.

It is our thoughts, feelings and behaviour that increase the level of pressure we experience and cause anxiety. By following the ideas in this book you will feel the right amount of pressure to deal with an exam. I will help you change your present ways of thinking, feeling and behaving with regards to exams, which, right now, may be so familiar to you that you label them as 'just being me' and, therefore, unchangeable.

Figure 1.1: the effect of pressure on performance

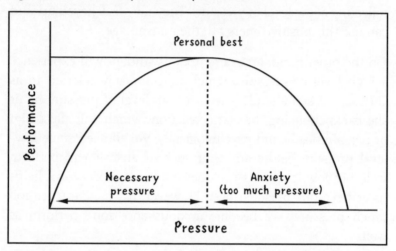

It may be hard to believe, but some people actually feel too *little* pressure at times, and therefore don't perform at their best. Take, for example, well-rehearsed actors before a performance. Professional actors have rehearsed exhaustively, right down to the detail of how they need to breathe at different parts of their performance. They often have to put on the same performance several times, even twice in one day. This can lead to them being too laid-back, which means they need to have mechanisms in place to recharge themselves and bring their pressure levels back to the top of the curve. In Japan, performers often undertake rituals that look like stomping before a performance, in order to increase their energy levels.

Sports coaches often give their team a good pep talk before a match to increase their level of pressure, while sports psychologists often help sportspeople deal with high levels of anxiety before a competition. In both cases, the goal is once again to stay at the top of the curve.

As you have learned, if you are anxious over a long period of time the alarm reaction settles into your body. Grace is an example of a student who made herself sick with anxiety over time, which resulted in her performing at less than her best.

Grace

Grace is doing a four-year degree. She has been anxious about school tests and exams for as long as she can remember, but still managed to perform reasonably well and received high enough results to get into university.

Grace is now in her third year of university study but is only doing second-year courses. This is because she was too sick to take her second-year exams last year. She developed an allergy that resulted in an itchy rash all over her body, something she has never experienced before. Her doctor told her that the rash was most likely caused by stress. Grace's immune system was unable to cope because she was so run down and her body was unable to counteract the constant high level of pressure that was being caused by several years of exam anxiety.

The doctor referred Grace to her university's counselling service, and although she was a rather reluctant client

Grace (cont'd)

at first (as exam-anxious students often are), she did discover the cause of her exam anxiety and learn to bring her pressure level back to the top of the curve so that she could do her best in future exams.

Are you chronically anxious or exam-phobic?

There are two types of students who get anxious over exams. One is the type of student who experiences anxiety about most things, including exams, and the other has a specific anxiety about exams but is otherwise not an anxious person.

The type of student who perceives threats in many situations is almost always in a state of high pressure. The alarm reaction is lurking insidiously inside their body at all times. This sort of student suffers from chronic anxiety; exams are just one extra thing to worry about and cope with. Andy is a typical example of a chronically anxious student.

Chronically anxious Andy

Anxious Andy has chronic anxiety. He worries that he is too fat and hates going to parties because he worries what people will think of him. He worries about his mother who seems very unhappy, and he worries about going to bed because he thinks he won't be able to sleep. To top it all off, he is also worried about exams.

Andy could do something about all this anxiety, but he doesn't. Instead, he walks around worrying and feeling anxious. He doesn't get enough sleep, suffers from cold sores, drinks too much, bites his nails and vomits before going into an exam.

The other type of exam-anxious student has a phobia of exams. This type of student is not chronically anxious but, for some reason, has a specific fear of exams. One such example is exam-phobic Phom.

Exam-phobic Phom

Phom is a social person, and generally looks after her health and body, but when it comes to exams, she completely falls apart. She tries to avoid them (which she can't), shakes with fright outside the exam room as she waits to go in and can't sleep the night before an exam. Phom is not usually an anxious sort of person, but, for some reason, she has a specific fear of exams. Phom needs to find out the reason for her fear so she can do something about it.

Do you know if you suffer from chronic anxiety or exam phobia? If you are unsure, the exercises in part II of this book will help you find out which one applies to your situation.

Chapter summary

In this chapter you have learned that:

⇨ the difference between fright and anxiety is whether or not a perceived threat is realistic

⇨ when we feel threatened we experience the alarm reaction, which is a physiological response that also affects us psychologically. When the threat goes away the response goes away, too, but if the threat remains the response settles into our body

⇨ we need some pressure to do well but if we have too much we get anxious and our performance level drops

⇨ there are two types of anxiety in relation to exams—some students get anxious about everything that is going on in their lives, while some only suffer from a specific fear of exams.

Chapter 2

Why students have different responses to exams

There are several factors that influence us over the course of our lives, such as heredity from our genes and unforeseen events. Another influence is our personality, which grows from birth (some say before birth) and develops as we mature. Personality is a major factor in differences between people, including different responses to exams. Heredity and unforeseen events cannot be changed, but it is possible to modify our personality so that it works *for* us rather than *against* us in exam situations.

There are many theories on personality, most saying the same thing in different ways. In my experience, students find it easiest to understand their exam anxiety by exploring the idea of personality being made up of three parts.

⇨ *Borrowed patterns* — these are the thoughts, feelings and behaviours we have 'borrowed' from important people in our lives. They are developed from all the actual and inferred messages we have received from these people over the course of our lives, particularly in early childhood. These messages can also be transmitted through the media and the internet.

⇨ *Child patterns* — these are the thoughts, feelings and behaviours that we experienced as a child, particularly as a young child, and that have developed further over the years.

⇨ *Adult insight* — this is the part of our personality that chooses what to use and what not to use from the above patterns in order to respond to current situations in an effective way. It is the last part of our personality to develop.

All three parts play a role in our life's 'script'. This is where our thoughts, feelings and behaviours are played out. We can say that our life's script has a basic plot, various acts and an ending, just like a play. But, unlike a play, we can influence our script if we want to. When people make personal changes to guide their script towards a positive end they are using their adult insight to make their borrowed and child patterns work for them rather than against them.

We will now explore the concepts of patterns and scripts in more detail.

Patterns

Let's start by exploring the patterns of a student called Annie to more fully understand the idea of borrowed and child patterns and the use of adult insight. We will be returning to Annie at several points in this chapter and she will also be used to illustrate some of the exercises later in the book.

Annie

Annie is a hardworking student but when it comes to exams she has huge difficulties. She is very scared of failing, despite the hard work she puts in to exam revision and throughout the school year. The closer an exam gets, the sicker Annie feels. She becomes very muddled in her thinking and cries a lot in private.

Annie's parents have often told her that in order to get a worthwhile job she has to do very well in her education and that in order to do well she must study very hard. They have also told her that graduates who get low marks might as well not have bothered with further study for all the good it does them.

These messages linking studying hard with getting a good job were repeatedly relayed to Annie when she was growing up, even when she was a young child. Annie can remember her mother's younger brother getting high marks in his final school exams and her parents being overjoyed and telling everyone that he would go on to get a great job after finishing university. They even bought him an expensive watch as a congratulatory present.

Because of Annie's belief that she needs high marks in order to pursue a worthwhile career, she studies hard. She enjoys doing her assignment and project work, takes her time with these tasks, and gets good marks.

Annie *(cont'd)*

But as her exams draw closer Annie starts to experience feelings of anxiety. She knows that she can't approach an exam like she does an assignment because of the time limit. She is scared that she won't get the good marks that will eventually lead to a worthwhile job, and she is also worried about disappointing her parents.

How do Annie's difficulties with exams translate into borrowed and child patterns? How could she use her adult insight? Let's first take a look at both types of patterns using Annie as an example.

Borrowed patterns

When we automatically think, feel and behave in ways that we have learned from our caregivers, without taking into account the reality of the current situation, we are using borrowed patterns. Of course, we usually do operate in ways that we have been taught. It is when we *automatically* take in the thoughts, feelings and behaviours of others and consider them our own, rather than *choosing* how we want to be as adults, that we are operating using borrowed patterns. As we grow through adolescence into adulthood our collection of borrowed patterns expands, containing all the social and psychological influences that we automatically operate from, rather than those that we choose to operate from. Our borrowed patterns are then expressed outwardly through our behaviour and inwardly through our thoughts and feelings.

Messages can be 'borrowed' from any significant person

In Annie's case, the anxiety-producing messages about having to do very well and study hard in order to get a good job came from her parents; however, borrowed messages and their resulting patterns don't have to come from parents. They can come from anyone who has had an influence on us over the course of our lives. Other than our parents, people who impart strong messages could be older siblings, teachers, examiners, adult friends of the family, ministers of religion, grandparents or members of our extended family, peers, or even sporting coaches. These people most likely nurtured or controlled us in some way. We may have happy memories of these people or may remember them with feelings of anger, fear or sadness. Remember: we take on messages from influential people believing them to be our own. In Annie's case she, too, believes she needs to do well in her studies to get a good job. But does this belief come directly from her own thinking, or has she taken her parents' thinking on board? And even if she has adopted her parents' opinions, is this a bad thing? Taking on useful messages will be explored later with the explanation of adult insight.

Care-giving behaviour is not always good for us

Some borrowed patterns are very positive but some can be negative, even if this was not the message-giver's intention. In Annie's case her parents were probably trying to do the right thing by her and didn't mean to make Annie feel so threatened by exams. It is important to emphasise that caregivers are usually trying to help us when giving us messages about study—or anything else, for that matter. Most of them are doing their best to help us grow up, but communication is a two-way event and, whatever the message, when we are young we interpret what we hear with our equally young brain.

The case of Danny illustrates this point well.

Danny

Danny's mother often praised him when he was young by saying he did so well 'for Mummy'. Through counselling, Danny began to understand that he had interpreted his mother's praise so literally with his young brain that he had since decided that the only way to get ahead in life was to do well 'for Mummy'. By the time he got to college he was very anxious about exams because he thought that if he didn't do well his mother would be upset with him. This borrowed message grew as he grew and ended up being not very useful.

By the end of his counselling sessions Danny realised that his mother was trying to do the right thing but that her praise had misfired through no fault of her own. He went to his next exam knowing that his mother may or may not get upset if he failed, and that even if she did get upset, it was her problem, not his. He discarded his borrowed pattern and chose a much healthier one for himself.

Danny's case illustrates that as a child we can interpret messages in ways other than those our caregivers intended. It is worth emphasising that most caregivers provide lots of good messages as we grow up; however, we need to acknowledge that some caregivers certainly *do not* do their best to help children grow up into psychologically healthy individuals. Children who are abused sexually, emotionally or physically can grow up with very negative messages and the patterns forming their personality can be extremely unhealthy. For example, if Annie's parents had shouted at her or even hit her when she didn't get high marks, or if they forced her to stay in her room to study, then the message about having to do well to get a good job would have been given in a very unhealthy way.

Psychologists and counsellors now know that messages can often be passed down from generation to generation, unless someone in the chain is able to change their patterns. So if Annie was physically and emotionally abused in order to make her work hard, then she could well raise her own children in the same way. Using the same argument, it could be that one, or both, of Annie's parents were also parented in an unhealthy way as far as studying is concerned. We can become trapped within our patterns and pass them on if we are not willing to change, and remember: we *can* change if we want to.

By now you should be able to see that although we can observe someone's behaviour, we can't understand their thoughts and feelings until we get to know them better. We have to talk to them, often at length, to uncover their thoughts and true feelings and, therefore, what drives their behaviour. With an exam-anxious person we can often tell that they are anxious (by what they say, how they act and what they look like), but we will have little idea about their thoughts and feelings towards exams until we get to know them better. Also, exam-anxious students can't understand their own anxiety about exams until they get to know themselves better. Unravelling our child patterns can often help with this.

Child patterns

When we think, feel and behave in ways that are a repetition of how we did in the past (usually as far back as our childhood) without taking into account the reality of the current situation, then we are said to be using our child patterns. Child patterns usually contribute to our thoughts and feelings more so than our behaviour. When we experience an unexpected stab of a feeling—for example, anger, fear, shame, or even pleasure—it may well originate from childhood feelings.

Let's examine Annie's problems with exams further.

Annie

As we now know, Annie was given repeated messages to do well academically. Some of these messages were indirect; for example, 'doing well leads to getting an expensive present'. Over the years Annie learnt from these messages that her parents would only be pleased with her if she got excellent results—the way to please them was to do well. As far as her child patterns were concerned, she also learned that if she did not get high marks she would not get a good job and her parents would be furious, which was very scary. If she had been abused in the past for not doing well her parents' fury would be even more threatening.

So, as she grew up Annie started to feel very anxious about exams because the stakes were so high. Her anxiety took the form of feeling nauseous, experiencing muddled thinking and crying in private.

If she didn't do well enough her parents would be very disappointed and even angry. Today, when Annie has an exam approaching, she starts to feel the same symptoms of anxiety she felt when she was younger. When this happens she is operating from child patterns.

Dealing with our childhood messages

By now you will have a basic understanding of borrowed and child patterns. You might even see how they can work in tandem to cause problems. In Annie's case her borrowed patterns were full of messages about having to do well in exams and her child patterns were full of anxiety about not doing well.

There are different ways of reacting to childhood messages. Some of us conform to them, some withdraw and others rebel. We also react differently according to the person who is influencing us and to different types of messages.

Imagine a situation where a teacher is known to humiliate children in front of the class if they get the answer to a question wrong. A conforming child might adapt to the teacher's behaviour by answering the question but may still experience feelings of dread that they will get the answer wrong. A withdrawing child might be unwilling to answer the question because they prefer to put up with the teacher's anger at their silence rather than be embarrassed in front of the class if they get the answer wrong. A rebellious child may speak up but be rude, and even throw a temper tantrum, or they might throw paper aeroplanes behind the teacher's back.

However we choose to deal with our childhood messages, we are forming patterns of behaviour that we will likely take with us on our journey into adulthood. The child who conforms may become a passive adult, the child who withdraws may become a 'silent type', and the child who rebels may turn into an aggressive adult.

In the case study of Annie, she cried in private, which was her way of withdrawing. She could continue this behaviour as an adult, without ever thinking about different ways of dealing with the situation.

By now you might be thinking that borrowed and child patterns do not necessarily have to be so problematic. What's wrong with being childlike and having fun? And going back to the example of Annie, isn't it good that she's aiming high? What about positive parenting? If Annie's parents encourage her to do well in a loving way, then surely that can't be a bad thing. The answers to all these questions have to do with choice, a concept that is central to the third part of our personality, adult insight.

Adult insight

Our adult insight is not driven by the past; rather, it is a way of thinking that encourages us to respond to a given situation in an appropriate way rather than from unconscious child or borrowed patterns. The concept of choice is central here. We might choose to use some child or borrowed patterns to deal with a particular situation but we would only be choosing useful aspects of these historical patterns to work for us in the present by integrating them into our adult insight for the task at hand.

For example, if you are crossing the road you would probably look right, left and right again before crossing, particularly if it was busy. Most likely someone taught you to cross the road in this way, and as an adult you have chosen to integrate this past borrowed pattern into your adult insight in order to stay safe.

If you heard some sad news and cried you would also be acting from your adult insight because you were, in fact, sad, even though crying is a childlike behaviour. Crying when you are sad is a healthy response. If, however, you tried to hold back the tears because 'big boys don't cry', then you would be operating from a negative borrowed pattern.

If we allow our thoughts, feelings and behaviour to help, rather than hinder, us, then we are successfully integrating the past into the present to help us deal with the current situation. Of course, the 'choice' is usually more or less instantaneous; we don't stop to ponder our every thought, feeling or action. For example, we probably wouldn't consciously stop and think about whether we should allow ourselves to cry or not.

Let's go back again to Annie and her exam problems.

Annie

What would happen if Annie operated from her adult insight? To know this, we firstly have to understand what Annie's goals are, rather than what her parents' goals are for her, although they could be the same.

Let's assume that Annie has decided she wants to be an architect. Using her adult insight Annie would talk to

Annie *(cont'd)*

a career adviser, and she might find out that a career in architecture suits her own interests and values, and that her particular strengths and aptitudes mean the goal of becoming an architect is reasonable. Her next task would be to gather the facts she needs in order to decide on the best avenue of study to achieve her goal.

Armed with this information, Annie's adult insight could make an informed decision about her career path, and it would be her decision, not her parents'. Of course, she may decide to talk it over with her parents, but the final decision would be hers. In fact, if she is using her adult insight Annie would probably consult with a number of people and perhaps even discover an alternative route to becoming a qualified architect in case her marks were not high enough—for example, another course that is a prerequisite for an architecture degree.

Using her adult insight, Annie would know that she needs to work hard and that she is prepared to do so. At the same time, she would also make sure that she didn't work at a level that was detrimental to her physical and mental wellbeing. Instead, she would find ways of managing her stress so that she could keep up the level of study required. She might join a yoga class, play sport regularly, eat well, make sure she got enough sleep and have a financial plan to get her through to the end of her training. She would also keep reminding herself that she was doing enough hard work to get good marks.

By doing all the things mentioned above Annie would be operating with her adult insight. As a consequence, she would have felt the twinge of anticipation and pressure to help her perform to the best of her ability, but she would not be experiencing the anxiety that would push her over the top of her curve, making her performance drop. She would not become nauseous or experience muddled thinking. Annie would be confronting any obstacles head on, rather than crying about them.

Adult insight doesn't equal boring

You may be thinking that to live your life using your adult insight sounds extremely boring. This is not so! Remember: we can also use the thoughts, feelings and behaviour that we learned in the past if we choose to do so. We can have fun using our positive child patterns. On the other hand, we can also experience sad or angry feelings even though we are operating with our adult insight. For example, we cry when we feel sad and get angry about injustices to ourselves, others, or the world.

No-one is perfect

People who operate using adult insight all the time sound too perfect—and that's because they are! No-one can use adult insight *all* the time, but people who try to use their adult insight in their life more often than not tend to be successful in whatever it is they are striving for.

I mentioned earlier that our borrowed and child patterns and our adult insight play a part in developing our life's script. It is now time to explore the concept of scripts, because it is your script that drives your exam anxiety and makes you feel stressed out.

Scripts

Patterns, when acted out in a script, play a big part in making one person different from another. Just like actors have to learn, rehearse and then perform a stage script, all of us 'learn' through the words and actions of others and the world at large (particularly when we are children), and through our own thoughts, feelings and behaviours. We also 'learn' through events that happen to us, through reading, and through our fantasies and dreams. We then go on to 'perform' what we have learned. We can think about our script being 'written' by the time we are about seven, 'revised' in later childhood and 'performed' in adulthood.

Let's look at the example of Damian to illustrate the ideas of learning, revising and performing a script.

Damian

When Damian was growing up and learning various childhood tasks, such as tying his shoelaces and saying 'thank you', his parents made a big deal of praising him when he did well and showing their displeasure when he did badly. For this reason, as a young child Damian 'learned' that if he did well his parents would be happy.

As an adolescent Damian tried to do well at school, because he knew that if he did, Mum and Dad would be pleased. Indeed, they were overjoyed when he won a school prize, as was his teacher. At school Damian was 'revising' his script when he worked out that doing well academically also brought happiness to others. In adulthood, and as a student, Damian 'performed' his script of needing to do well by studying far too long and hard because he thought marks were everything so he mustn't have a social life. He pushed himself too hard and got very stressed out.

It is now time for you to learn how and why we maintain our script, even when it takes us in a direction that we don't want to be heading. It is important to understand that your script *can* be changed to allow your life to work well for you; or in this case, to help you deal with your anxiety about exams.

Scripts are maintained unless we change our act

Because we are vulnerable and dependent when we are young, we take in the messages told to us or that we have inferred. By the time we are about seven years old our borrowed and child patterns are becoming fairly stable and we start to build a view of the world and our place in it. We also start to have expectations of the world and, more importantly, look for ways of maintaining these expectations. Let's use Sol as an example.

Sol

Sol is the youngest in a family of three boys. His two brothers tended to play together when they were growing up because they were closer in age. In the first seven years or so of his life, Sol tried to keep up with them but couldn't because he was too young. When he tried to do the things they were doing, such as building things in the backyard or reading books, he could never do them as well, so his brothers teased him and called him 'Stupid Sol'. By the time he was about seven, Sol thought he was stupid and that others were cleverer than he was. He felt ashamed of himself.

During his later childhood, Sol decided that he didn't want to join in activities at school because he thought people would realise how stupid he was. The thought of this happening caused a knot to form in his stomach. In this way he was refining his script. By the time he reached adulthood, Sol used his script to rationalise situations. For example, when his wife told him that they shouldn't go on a skiing holiday he immediately thought she was against the idea because she thought he was too stupid to learn to ski and that they would therefore be wasting their money. In fact, she was against the idea because her sister was having a baby and she wanted to be around her to support her. She had even told him this on more than one occasion.

Sol's misunderstanding of the situation is an example of how he maintains a script started in childhood to this day.

We need to think of our script being perpetuated by a system that we have set up for ourselves, even though we have done so subconsciously. To further understand why you continue to stress out over exams you need to understand your own script system, which you will have the opportunity of doing in the next chapter.

Script systems

Using the previous case study of Sol, we can think of our script system as being made up of four parts:

⇨ our outward behaviours (Sol tried not to put himself in a position where his perceived stupidity would show)

⇨ our internal bodily experiences (each time Sol thought he was going to be 'found out' he got a knot in his stomach)

⇨ our reinforcing memories and fantasies (Sol often remembered his brothers telling him that he was stupid and fantasised about their reactions if they heard that he was considering a skiing holiday)

⇨ our beliefs and feelings about ourselves, others and the world in general (Sol thought he was stupid, that others were smarter than he was, and that people in general despised stupid people).

As it is a system, all parts influence each other. Figure 2.1 (overleaf) explains how the process works. This figure is adapted from the racket system devised by Erskine and Zalcman. (See further reading for more information.)

Figure 2.1: how a script system works

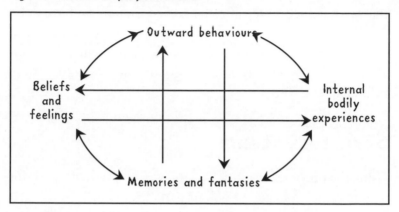

Following is a brief summary of the common reactions experienced for each aspect of the script system.

Beliefs and feelings

An exam-anxious student might think any of the following thoughts:

⇨ my life won't be worth living unless I pass (about themselves)

⇨ people will only love me if I am successful (about others)

⇨ everyone despises people without an education (about the world).

Outward behaviours

How does an exam-anxious person behave? Perhaps they:

⇨ put things off

⇨ are irritable

⇨ are forgetful

⇨ can't sleep.

Internal bodily experiences

An exam-anxious person may experience any of the following internal symptoms:

⇨ heart palpitations

⇨ an upset stomach

⇨ sore muscles

⇨ high blood pressure.

Reinforcing memories and fantasies

Memories are thoughts that we have when we remember something that actually happened in the past. Fantasies are thoughts that we have when we think about what could have happened in the past or what might happen in the future. An exam-anxious person might:

⇨ remember how ashamed they felt when they failed an exam

⇨ remember a significant person telling them that they were hopeless

⇨ fantasise about friends not wanting to hang out with them if they fail

⇨ fantasise about harming themselves in some way if they fail.

Let's use the case of Ross to further illustrate the concept of a script system. Remember that each of the four parts influences the other three.

Ross

From childhood Ross was known as the 'non-academic child' and was frequently told by his parents and two older siblings that he was a loser. He could never seem to get it right. After a while his reports came home from school saying things like 'Ross could do better', or 'Ross isn't working to his full potential'. He soon came to believe he was a loser and would never get far academically.

Ross knew his parents were disappointed in him. Exams were a nightmare and he got very anxious about them, but he did not seek help for his anxiety. He thought that when he failed, others would realise that he was not very clever. He started playing up at school, and he felt so tense inside that he started drinking with his mates when he was far too young.

Ross managed a year 12 score high enough to get him into a course at TAFE. He would have preferred to go to university but his score wasn't high enough. Even so, he didn't feel confident about successfully completing his TAFE course — he felt like a fraud and thought that he would never earn a big enough income. Ross's two older siblings had already managed to get into university — a fact that was never far from his mind.

Ross found the course hard, but instead of trying to complete it successfully by getting help from the college counsellor about his exam anxiety he started telling himself that he wasn't going to pass because he was a loser. He didn't study and the inevitable happened — he failed the course. Ross had often worried that he would end up stacking shelves in the local supermarket, and that's exactly what happened.

What do you think was in Ross's script, and how do you think he was maintaining it through his script system? From the information above we know that:

⇨ Ross was telling himself he was a loser, that others were disappointed in him and that in order to be rich he would have to get higher qualifications (beliefs and feelings about himself, others and the world)

⇨ he got involved with a crowd that was a bad influence on him, started drinking at an early age and didn't seek help for his exam anxiety (behaviour)

⇨ he felt very tense (internal bodily experiences)

⇨ he worried about getting a shelf-stacking job and often remembered that his two elder siblings had been accepted to university (memories and fantasies).

Can you see how all these parts of Ross's script system interacted with each other to keep his system going? He made sure that he could keep telling himself, 'Well, there you are, I told you I was a loser'.

Annie

For a look at another example of a script system, let's return to an earlier case study, Annie, and see what is in her script system and how she maintains it:

- Annie thinks she will never get high enough marks, that others will get better marks and that in order to succeed you have to do well academically (beliefs and feelings about herself, others and the world)
- she cries in private (behaviour)
- she feels nauseous as exams approach (internal bodily experiences)
- she fantasises about ending up in a low-paid job and remembers her parents buying her uncle an expensive watch when he did well in his exams (memories and fantasies).

As you can see, all the parts of Annie's script system are affecting the other parts. She is on one big roller-coaster ride to a miserable life in terms of a job and success; that is, unless she lets her adult insight take over and steer her script towards a happier life.

Putting patterns and scripts together

You can now understand that the content of our patterns and scripts forms a big part of our personality. Let's explore how these concepts work together by using Sam as an example.

Sam

Sam is 18 years old and facing his first exams at university. He has a history of being anxious about exams but has always managed to pass well enough to continue his schooling and get into university — although he doesn't think he is clever enough to be there. He has always put his results down to 'just good luck'. A friend took Sam to the university's counselling service just before Sam's afternoon exam because he was very worried about him. Sam was in a panic, had been up all night studying and kept saying, 'I can't do it'. He said his mind was a blank and he was trembling with fright — or possibly from drinking too much coffee.

The counsellor discovered that Sam had attended all his classes and handed in all his assignments, although some were late. Sam studies with friends and thought they all knew and understood much more than he did. He also has an older sister who completed university with no difficulties. His parents are expecting him to follow in her footsteps and are supporting him financially (which is a struggle) so that he doesn't have to get a part-time job and can spend more time studying. After all, he must be successful at university to get on in life. Sam feels like everyone is watching him to see if he will succeed like his sister did. He doesn't think he will. He doesn't think he is 'good enough'.

So what are Sam's borrowed and child patterns and how is he maintaining his script? From what we have to go on, it seems that Sam's borrowed patterns include his beliefs that he must do well in order to please his parents and that he is not 'good enough' academically. He tells himself, 'I must do well like my sister did'. This message is reinforced by the fact that his parents are putting themselves out to help him do well because, as he sees it, 'I need all the help I can get'. He also has been taught to believe that 'success is best'. Sam's child patterns are ones of panic, a feeling he used to experience as a child when he felt like he wasn't good enough. We can also surmise that he is running his script system with thoughts such as 'I am not good enough', 'Others are better than me' and 'It is best to be at the top'. He reminds himself that his parents are putting themselves out to make sure he does well and fantasises that his results to date have been due to good luck rather than his ability and hard work. He trembles with fright and his mind goes blank before an exam. This panic feeds all his beliefs, memories, fantasies, outward behaviour and internal bodily experiences, and they in turn all feed off each other. What a mess!

You may be wondering what the counsellor did in this situation. As Sam turned up just before his exam was due to start, she could only help him by using some of the tips on the first-aid page at the front of this book—there was no time to do anything else. Fortunately, Sam agreed to come back to see the counsellor early in the next semester, and when he did she went through the longer process of helping him to understand his patterns and script system in relation to exams. He also learned to use his adult insight to alter the direction of his script and went on to be a reasonably successful student.

Chapter summary

In this chapter you have learned that:

⇨ there are three parts of our personality that have a major role in our script formation, which can include being anxious about exams. These are:

- our borrowed patterns, which are developed from all the actual and inferred messages that we have received from significant people and the media over the years, particularly our early years

- our child patterns, which are developed from our thoughts, feelings and behaviours as a child, particularly as a young child

- our adult insight, which can work positively to guide our script towards a successful outcome, including not being stressed out over exams

⇨ our script develops unconsciously when we are young, and may remain that way unless we realise that we are repeating patterns we have learned in childhood and revised in adolescence. Our adult insight can change these patterns

⇨ our script system maintains our script and has four parts — behaviour, internal bodily experiences, memories and fantasies and beliefs and feelings. All four parts influence each other

⇨ we have to become aware of and understand our patterns and script system in order to change them. Chapter 3 will help you do this.

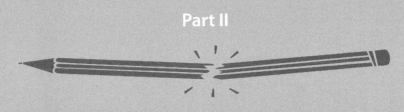

Why do I get anxious about exams?

I don't want the peace which passeth understanding. I want the understanding which bringeth peace.

—Helen Keller (1880–1968)

Part II of this book has only one chapter. By doing the exercises in it you will find out what your borrowed and child patterns are and how much you tend to use your adult insight. You will also identify what is in your script and how your script system operates to maintain your script as far as your exam anxiety is concerned.

Do the exercises as thoughtfully and honestly as you can. You will need a notebook for some sections to write down your answers. They're not exam questions and no-one needs to see your answers. By doing these exercises you may find you start thinking about your earlier life in ways you never have before, or you may find yourself out of your comfort zone. If this happens to you, then you are most likely unearthing the very issues that make you so stressed out about exams—what a step forward!You will find plenty of relevant ideas and hints in the remainder of the book to help you conquer this anxiety.

On the other hand, you may find that being out of your comfort zone is too hard, or that you are discovering parts of yourself or your past that are too upsetting or confronting. If this is the case then I suggest that you talk to an understanding friend or a counsellor at your educational institution before completing the exercises. It is certainly not my intention to make you upset, but I do want to help you find out more about yourself in terms of your exam anxiety. First you need to understand, then you can fix the problem.

Chapter 3

Discovering the causes of your exam anxiety

This chapter is filled with exercises that will help you discover the cause, or causes, of your anxiety towards exams. To do these exercises successfully you will need to use two skills from time to time. These are centering and grounding.

Centering

Centering yourself is a means of relaxing. It is not the same as doing something relaxing, such as reading a good book or going for a swim, but it is a way of quietening your body, both internally and externally. As your body relaxes, your breathing will become slower and your pulse will slow down. You can move from the alarm reaction, described in chapter 1, to a very low level of physical and psychological pressure. Track 2 on the CD teaches you how to do this. Listen to it. Basic instructions on how to centre yourself are also provided in the box below for a quick reference.

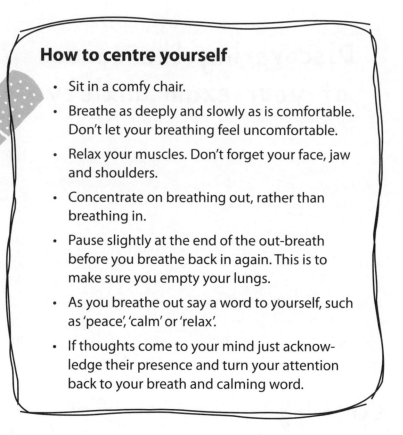

How to centre yourself

- Sit in a comfy chair.

- Breathe as deeply and slowly as is comfortable. Don't let your breathing feel uncomfortable.

- Relax your muscles. Don't forget your face, jaw and shoulders.

- Concentrate on breathing out, rather than breathing in.

- Pause slightly at the end of the out-breath before you breathe back in again. This is to make sure you empty your lungs.

- As you breathe out say a word to yourself, such as 'peace', 'calm' or 'relax'.

- If thoughts come to your mind just acknowledge their presence and turn your attention back to your breath and calming word.

Grounding

After finishing an exercise, or if you wish to stop in the middle of one, it helps if you 'ground' yourself. Grounding is a means of helping you to be in the present and feel strong. The term comes from phrases such as 'having your feet firmly on the ground' or 'not being a pushover'. Grounding is a particularly useful technique to use if you have been thinking about the past, as it brings your focus back to the present moment. I will remind you to ground yourself after exercises that ask you to think about your past.

How to ground yourself:

⇨ Stand up, spread your toes and feel the ground under your feet.

⇨ Find a sense of balance.

⇨ Look around you and be aware of where you are.

⇨ Tell yourself what year it is.

⇨ Tell yourself what day of the week it is.

⇨ Tell yourself what the time is.

⇨ Move around the room.

⇨ If thoughts come to mind about an exercise just acknowledge the thoughts and let them go.

⇨ Focus on what you are doing in the here and now.

Now, with these two techniques in mind, let's move on to the exercises and start your journey of self-discovery by uncovering and exploring your borrowed patterns.

Finding your borrowed patterns

There are two exercises to help you discover your borrowed patterns. The first addresses your borrowed patterns in general, while the second is specific to exam anxiety.

In order to find out about your borrowed patterns you will need to become as aware as possible of how your influential parental figures thought, felt and behaved when you were growing up. Remember, these parental figures could be your actual parents, but could also be people who made a significant impact on you, in either a positive or a negative way.

Exercise 1: discovering your borrowed patterns

This exercise has three parts and will take about 20 to 30 minutes of uninterrupted time to complete. It will ask you to think about your past, so if you need to, stop doing the exercise mid-way so you can ground yourself and then continue when you are ready. Part A invites you to remember how your influential people behaved and how you believe they thought and felt. Part B asks you to consider how *you* behave, think and feel now. Part C invites you to reflect on similarities between the influential people in your past and yourself in the present.

Part A: thinking about influential people in your past

Firstly, choose the two most influential people in your life up to about the age of eight (you will have a chance to choose another influential person in the next exercise).

Now sit back in a comfy chair and relax, and follow the instructions on page 42 to centre yourself (or listen to track 2 on the CD).

Once you are feeling relaxed, take a few deep breaths and try to remember a setting, such as home, school, or some other place where you were with each of these influential people. It could be the same place for both of them, or two different places. If you choose a home and have lived in more than one, you may need to remember each home separately.

There is no right or wrong way to do this exercise. The point is to try and remember what your early life was like with these people, so just adapt my instructions to fit your own situation. It is also important to remember that people's ability to remember their childhood varies, and it might be that you do not remember very much at all. Don't worry if you can't remember a lot or if you can't answer all the questions. You will still get some insights from the exercise.

Once you have a clear picture in your mind of life back then, answer the following questions. Because your answers may be different for each person it may help to answer the questions for each person individually.

1   How did each person act when they were:

    a   angry?

    b   happy?

    c   sad?

    d   scared?

    e   ashamed?

2   How did each person cope with their job (if they had one)?

3   What did each person think about their friends' jobs?

4   How did each person respond to a crisis (for example, death, job loss or illness)?

5   If you ate meals with each person, what was the atmosphere like when you ate together?

6   Did you feel that each person listened to you?

7   What were each person's mannerisms?

8   What did each person think about your formal education?

9   How would each person describe the perfect child?

10 How would each person describe you?

Once you've finished answering the questions for each person, write some key reminder words in the first two columns of table 3.1 and then get up and ground yourself.

Part B: thinking about you

When you are ready, answer the questions below in relation to yourself at the current point in time. Then, add some key words to the final column of table 3.1.

1   How do you act when you are:

    a   angry?

    b   happy?

    c   sad?

    d   scared?

    e   ashamed?

2   How do you cope with your job (if you have one)?

3   What do you think about your friends' jobs?

4   How do you respond to a crisis (for example, death, job loss or illness)?

5   What is the atmosphere like when you eat with others?

6   Do you listen to others?

7 What are your mannerisms?

8 What do you think about your formal education?

9 How would you describe the perfect child?

10 How would you describe yourself?

Table 3.1: keywords as reminders

Item	Person A (Fill in after completing part A)	Person B (Fill in after completing part A)	Me (Fill in after completing part B)
1a			
b			
c			
d			
e			
2			
3			
4			
5			
6			
7			

Table 3.1 *(cont'd)*: keywords as reminders

Item	Person A	Person B	Me
8			
9			
10			

Part C: making connections to understand your borrowed patterns

By looking at the words you have written above, answer the following questions to discover any similarities between yourself and the two significant people from your past.

⇨ Are any of the answers relating to either of the influential figures in part A similar to the answers relating to you in part B? If so, which ones?

⇨ What do you think about these similarities? For example, are you surprised, happy or sad?

As a result of doing this exercise you should start to become aware of the ways of behaving, and perhaps even thinking and feeling, that you have borrowed from the influential people in your life. Remember: borrowing can be positive and it might be that your adult insight makes good use of the patterns you have borrowed. But it might also mean that you don't want to use some or all of these borrowed patterns any longer.

The next exercise will help you decide which of these patterns you want to keep and which ones you want to discard. In particular, we will be looking at your borrowed patterns in areas related to success and exams.

Exercise 2: discovering your borrowed patterns related to exam anxiety

This exercise has six parts, but you don't need to do them all at once. You might like to take a break between each part and have a think about your answers to that point. Remember: there are no right or wrong answers. The aim is for you to work out what your borrowed patterns are (those that you have taken in as though they were your own thoughts), and what *you* think using your adult insight. In this exercise I am asking you to make decisions that you may find difficult, but what you'll find out about yourself as a result of doing this exercise will be invaluable as far as getting rid of your exam anxiety is concerned. I have given you examples along the way and occasionally I have used Annie, from chapter 2, in order to provide further examples. Annie's answers are given in italics, and to make it simple I have used only two of Annie's statements. If Annie were doing the exercise herself she would have found many more relevant statements.

The answers to parts A, C, D and a section of part of E are to be written in table 3.2 (overleaf). The answers to parts B, F and the remainder of part of E are to be written in your notebook.

Part A: identifying general statements about success and associated areas that you heard when you were younger

In the spaces provided in the top row of table 3.2 write the names of three people who influenced you in the first eight years or so of your life. You have already chosen two people in exercise 1, so you just have to think of one more.

Table 3.2: exercise to discover how your borrowed patterns relate to exam anxiety

Area for comment	Examples	Person A	Person B	Person C	Part C	Part D	Part E
Achieving success	• Getting to the top of the ladder is best.				A	A	A
	• If at first you don't succeed, try again.				B	B	B
					C	C	C
Education	• It's better to be a happy truck driver than an unhappy doctor.				A	A	A
	• It is important to get a degree.				B	B	B
					C	C	C

Area for comment	Examples	Person A	Person B	Person C	Part C	Part D	Part E
Study	• Only people who study hard are successful.				A	A	A
	• Studying is only for foolish people.				B	B	B
					C	C	C
Exams	• Exams sort the fainthearted from the strong.				A	A	A
	• Exams are a necessity.				B	B	B
					C	C	C
Careers	• Career changes are disastrous.				A	A	A
	• It's okay to change careers.				B	B	B
					C	C	C

Under each person's name see if you can write a *general statement* (or two) that the person would say (or has said) about the following five areas: achieving success, education, study, exams and careers. These could be either positive or negative statements. The aim is to try to remember what general statements each person made about each area, but not necessarily about you in particular, although you may well think the statements also applied to you. You may find that people are not consistent and have given different or contradictory messages at different times. If so, write the statement that seems most influential. Some examples of typical statements are given in the first column to help you understand the exercise.

Part B: thinking about these statements

The questions below are to help you think more about part A. Write your answers in your notebook.

Can you see a theme (or themes) to the statements?

Annie could write that 'studying hard leads to a good job', and 'it's best to get to the top of the ladder'.

Were you influenced by any of these statements?

Annie might write that she was influenced by both statements.

Who influenced you in this way?

Annie might say that it was her parents or perhaps a teacher.

Were they positive or negative influences?

Annie may be unsure if they were positive or negative influences.

Is there anything so far that surprises you? If so, what does?

Annie may be surprised to realise just how hard her parents, and perhaps others, have pushed her to study.

Part C: discovering which statements you agree with

Go back to table 3.2 and the sentences that you have written for part A of the exercise. Think about whether you agree with any of them. In the column on the table headed 'part C', put a tick next to the corresponding person who made a general statement that you agree with. If you don't agree with a statement then don't put a tick for that person. For example, if you agree with a general statement that person A made about achieving success, then put a tick against the letter 'A' in the corresponding box in the column for part C. Do this for all three people and for all five areas for comment. Be really honest with yourself.

Included in Annie's ticked general statements may be 'Only those who study hard are successful', and 'Getting to the top of the ladder is best'.

Part D: finding out if the statements applied to you

We are now on the path to finding your borrowed patterns. So far we have been identifying general statements, and the next step is to see if you believe these statements were meant for you. For each general statement you have ticked under the column for part C (because you agree with it), try saying the statement out loud as an 'I should' or an 'I must' statement. You may need to reword the sentence to do this; just make sure you don't change the meaning behind it. For example, if a person you have chosen said (or says), 'Getting to the top of the ladder is best', then say out loud, 'I *should* get to the top of the ladder'. If they said (or say) 'exams sort the fainthearted from the strong', then say out loud 'I *should* be strong' or 'I *must* be strong'. Remember, you are only doing this for the statements you have ticked under part C.

Do you agree with what you are saying out loud? Go to the column headed 'part D' and put a second tick against those that you still agree with after you have turned them into 'I should' or 'I must' statements. By now some statements will have two ticks against them.

Annie might say, 'I must study hard in order to get a good job', or 'I should get to the top of the ladder'. She might also have put a second tick against these statements because by turning them into 'I should' or 'I must' statements, she felt as though they were meant for her.

Part E: identifying statements you would like your adult insight to use

Look over the sentences you have ticked under the column for part D. Rather than a 'should' or 'must' statement, try saying the statements out loud as an 'I *want*' statement, and at the same time think about your forthcoming exams. For example, 'I *want* to get to the top of the ladder' or 'I *want* to be strong'. Do the sentences really feel right to you? Do you feel comfortable saying these statements to the world? If you do feel comfortable with your 'I want' statements then give them a tick under the column marked 'part E'.

Now write down all the statements that feel right to you in your notebook. Make sure they are statements that feel accurate and useful—statements that you really want for yourself. If you are unsure, try saying the sentence to other people to double-check. If a statement feels right to you when you say it out loud you will probably want your adult insight to use that thinking when necessary. Another way to check is to ask yourself if you would want to pass this message on to your own child or to a child in your care. Some of the hints and exercises in the following chapter will help you to solidify these statements and make them work for you.

Annie may write that she wants to study hard to get a good job, but she may not write that she wants to get to the top of the ladder. She may have realised that this is not her goal, although it may have been the goal her parents set for her.

Part F: identifying the statements you want to disregard

Finally, write in your notebook any sentences that you ticked under the columns for part C and part D, but not for part E (they will have two ticks next to them). These are the statements that you have identified as meant for you but that you *don't* agree with. Most likely, these sentences contain the messages from your borrowed patterns to do with success, exams and related areas that you *don't* want your adult insight to use; in other words, statements that you *don't* want to relate to. These are the messages I am going to teach you to disregard, because they play a large part in making you anxious about exams.

Annie may write that she does not want to get to the top of her chosen profession.

Well done! You have now identified the borrowed patterns that you *don't* want your adult insight to use and those ideas that you *would* like your adult insight to use. Now that you know this, we can move on to identifying your child patterns.

Finding your child patterns

In order to get in touch with your child patterns, you need to become as aware as possible of how you thought, felt and behaved in the first eight years or so of your life. By doing so you will find out more about why you react so strongly exams. The next four exercises (3 to 6) are concerned with your child patterns in general, while the following two exercises (7 and 8) are concerned with your child patterns with regards to exams.

Exercise 3: childhood memories

This exercise has two parts. Part A asks you to relax and think about your childhood, particularly the home, or homes, that you lived in until you were about eight years of age. Remember that people's ability to remember their childhood varies and your aim is only to get as clear a picture as you can. If you feel uncomfortable at any time during the exercise, simply stop and ground yourself following the instructions provided earlier. Part B will ask you how you reacted to these memories.

Part A: remembering

Sit in a comfy chair, close your eyes and centre yourself (if you need to, listen to track 2 on the CD). When you are ready allow your mind to travel back in time to the house or houses you lived in until you were about eight (this may even be the house you are living in now). Try to see the house (or houses), hear any sounds that you may have heard when you lived there as a small child, smell any smells and taste any tastes that your memory brings back. If you lived in more than one house you may need your mind to travel through them one at a time. Notice your feelings as you do this exercise.

Once you have a good picture in your mind of your house back then, and of yourself in it, think about the following questions. You may not be able to answer all of them.

⇨ Who lived in the house with you?

⇨ What noises did you hear when in the house?

⇨ What smells did you smell when in the house?

⇨ What tastes did you taste when in the house?

⇨ Who was the dominant person in the house?

⇨ How did you feel towards this person?

⇨ Can you remember a happy time? If so, what happened? What did you think at the time?

⇨ Can you remember a sad time? If so, what happened? What did you think at the time?

⇨ Can you remember a time that you felt shame? If so, what happened? What did you think at the time?

⇨ Can you remember a time that you were afraid? If so, what happened? What did you think at the time?

⇨ Can you remember something that made you angry? If so, what was it? What did you think at the time?

⇨ What words best describe your time in this house (for example, happy, scared, angry, sad or ashamed)?

When you have finished answering these questions, ground yourself so that you are aware of where you are right now.

Part B: thinking about what you remember

As soon as possible after completing part A, answer the following questions in your notebook.

⇨ How did you feel as you did this exercise?

⇨ Were you surprised by what you remembered? If so, was it a pleasant or an unpleasant surprise?

⇨ What stood out for you?

⇨ What do you think your most common feeling was (for example, happiness, fear, anger, sadness or shame)?

⇨ What was the second most common feeling?

Exercise 4: looking at old photographs

Another way to connect with your childhood is to look at family photographs. If you have photos of yourself and your surroundings when you were young, take some time to get them out and think about what you see when you look at them. Here are some questions to think about while doing this.

⇨ Do the photographs show a happy, sad, frightening or angry atmosphere?

⇨ What was going on in your life at the time?

⇨ Are you showing any emotion in pictures of yourself?

⇨ If so, can you still relate to these emotions?

If you can pick out any themes to do with emotion, write them in your notebook.

Exercise 5: favourite stories or fantasies from childhood

As children, we often have fantasies we either carry around in our heads or play out alone, or with others. We often also have a favourite type of story that we ask to have read to us, read ourselves, or watch on TV, video or DVD. We might like stories that involve 'saving' a person or an animal, about danger, about science fiction or fantasy, or perhaps about people having fun.

Thinking about childhood fantasies or favourite stories can help us get in touch with our child patterns and also help us understand ourselves better in the present. Try finishing these sentences in your notebook. Do they help you understand your child patterns in the present?

⇨ When I was a child I used to fantasise about ...

⇨ This helps me understand why in the present I ...

⇨ When I was a child I enjoyed stories that were ...

⇨ This helps me understand why in the present I ...

Exercise 6: comparing childhood emotions with the ones you feel now

To understand your child patterns further it is useful to remember the type of emotions you felt as a child compared with the type of emotions you feel most regularly now.

There are many emotions we can feel on a daily basis. The ones I have picked out for the sake of this exercise are sadness, anger, fright, shame and happiness. There are, of course, degrees of intensity for each one. Use table 3.3 (overleaf) to estimate your most common feelings in your childhood and today. Imagine that all your feelings add up to 100 per cent and divide your feelings up into the relevant proportions.

For example, a student might decide after doing exercise 3 that they mainly felt anger as a child, followed closely by feelings of fear. This student may decide to give anger a rating of 40 per cent and fear a rating of 20 per cent. They would then divide the remaining 40 per cent in some way between sadness, happiness and shame. Lastly, they would decide if the ratio for these emotions was about the same in the present, or whether the percentages had changed over time.

Fill in the table below, remembering that it is hard to be objective about things such as this. There are no right or wrong answers; only guesswork is needed.

Table 3.3: comparison of feelings in childhood versus the present

Emotion	Childhood	Present
Sadness	___%	___%
Anger	___%	___%
Fright	___%	___%
Shame	___%	___%
Happiness	___%	___%
Total	**100%**	**100%**

How similar is your emotional make-up now to how it was in your childhood? Are there any surprises in your answers? If so, write them in your notebook.

After doing these exercises you will have a very good idea about how you felt as a child and what your child patterns most likely are as a result. We will now move on to your child patterns in relation to exams.

Exercise 7: identifying child patterns surrounding exams

This exercise will help you make connections between your current ways of thinking, feeling and behaving towards exams, and how you remembered yourself as a child.

Part A: identifying current thoughts, feelings and behaviour surrounding exams

In your notebook, write a few words or phrases that describe how you thought, felt and behaved in the lead-up to and/or during a recent exam. Annie's answers are given in italics to help you understand the exercise, but it is important that you think about your own thoughts, feelings and behaviours.

Annie thought that she was going to disappoint her parents, she felt nauseous and scared, and she cried a lot in private.

Part B: making connections with yourself as a child

In exercises 3 to 6 you were asked to think about yourself as a child and you have just been asked to write down how you think, feel and behave towards exams today. Look over your answers and try to make some connections between what you were like as a child and what you are like as far as exams are concerned today. Write your ideas in your notebook. By doing this you will understand which of your child patterns are operating when you get anxious about exams.

Exercises to connect with both borrowed and child patterns

The next two exercises will help you connect to both your borrowed and child patterns so you understand how they can work together.

Exercise 8: role-play talking to significant people in your life about exams

You may find this exercise makes you feel more uncomfortable than others. Read the instructions below and then decide — using your adult insight — if you wish to continue. Feel free to stop at any time and ground yourself.

In exercise 2 you were asked to pick three people who have influenced you, either positively or negatively. Take each of these people in turn and pretend that they are standing in front of you. One or more of these people may no longer be alive, and this may be upsetting for you. If so, take note of how you feel about doing this and move on through the exercise if you can. Imagine that you are telling the first person that you have an exam coming up. Talk to them about the exam — tell them how much work you have done for it, or perhaps how you are thinking and feeling about it. Now stop and take note of how you are feeling right now. Was it easy to tell them these things, or did you feel some negative emotion? If you did, what did you feel and what does this mean? Repeat the exercise with the other two people on your list.

In your notebook jot down anything you want to record from this exercise and, in particular, record the emotions you felt as you talked to these people.

You may recognise some old patterns from your childhood that make you quite uncomfortable. The rest of this book is going to fix these problematic patterns, so right now, why don't you take a break and do something enjoyable before you continue with more exercises.

Exercise 9: identifying how your borrowed and child patterns work together

Exercise 9 connects the content of your borrowed and child patterns. As you now know, these two patterns often work in tandem, often with disastrous results.

Remember Sam from chapter 2? His borrowed patterns included the belief that he was not good enough academically and his child patterns included panicking. No wonder that when exams came along he felt he had to prove himself and panicked. Returning to Annie again, her borrowed patterns told her that it is essential to do well in exams and her child patterns included feeling scared that she might not please her Mum and Dad.

Are your borrowed and child patterns working together to make life a misery for you around exam time? In your notebook write down the main borrowed and child patterns that are influencing your anxiety over exams.

How much adult insight are you currently using?

Now that you've identified your borrowed and child patterns the next step is to decide how well you are using your adult insight. Remember that our adult insight chooses to respond to the current reality of a situation in a beneficial way and it may take on useful borrowed and child patterns in order to do this. As far as exams are concerned, our adult insight picks and chooses the most beneficial way of thinking, feeling and behaving in order to stop us feeling so anxious about exams. In chapter 2 we looked at how Annie could use her adult insight to help her get rid of her exam anxiety (you might like to remind yourself of the ways she could do this).

You may find it hard to think about how you could call on your adult insight to make life easier for you around exam time, but don't worry—that's why you're reading this book! Try doing exercise 10 to get an idea of how much adult insight you are using right now.

Exercise 10: estimating the current level of adult insight you use when dealing with exams

It is important to think about how you would like to think, feel and behave towards exams and also about how much adult insight you are currently using to help you take your exams with no worries. Parts A and B of this exercise will help you do this.

Part A: how you want to think, feel and behave towards exams

Think about an exam you have coming up and call on your adult insight to realistically answer the following questions. Write your answers in your notebook.

⇨ What would I like to *think* about the exam?

⇨ How would I like to *feel* about the exam?

⇨ How would I like to *behave* in the lead-up to and during the exam?

Part B: estimating your current level of adult insight

On a scale of 0 to 10, with 0 meaning 'I am not currently thinking, feeling or behaving at all like my adult insight wants me to', and 10 meaning 'I am currently thinking, feeling and behaving exactly how my adult insight wants me to', where would you rate yourself at this point in time?

My adult insight rating: _____

If you gave yourself a low score, don't panic! By the time you have finished this book you will be much closer to 10.

It is now time to look at what is in your script and how your script system is working to maintain it.

Figuring out your script and its system

You learnt about scripts in chapter 2. You may need to go back to this chapter and remind yourself about scripts and the concept of a script system before doing the next exercise.

Exercise 11: identifying the content of your script and how you maintain it

In part A of this exercise you are going to identify what is in your own script system as far as exams and related issues are concerned. In part B you will be able to figure out how you are maintaining your script, and therefore your anxiety towards your exams.

Part A: finding out the content of your script system around the issue of exams

Figure 3.1 shows the script system again.

Figure 3.1: script system

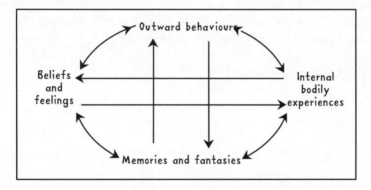

In your notebook, write down the contents of *your* system as far as exams and related areas are concerned. You identified most of the content of your script system in earlier exercises so this shouldn't be too hard. Write down your beliefs and feelings in relation to the following:

- yourself
- others
- the world.

In your notebook, also make note of the following:

- your memories about exams
- your fantasies about exams

- your outward behaviours at exam time
- your internal bodily experiences at exam time.

Part B: how you maintain your script system

By now there should not be any big surprises in your script system. But is your way of maintaining it becoming clearer? In your notebook, try completing the sentences below.

My beliefs and feelings influence my:

⇨ memories and fantasies by ...

⇨ outward behaviour by ...

⇨ internal bodily experiences by ...

My memories and fantasies influence my:

⇨ outward behaviour by ...

⇨ internal bodily experiences by ...

⇨ beliefs and feelings by ...

My outward behaviour influences my:

⇨ internal bodily experiences by ...

⇨ beliefs and feelings by ...

⇨ memories and fantasies by ...

My internal bodily experiences influence my:

⇨ beliefs and feelings by ...

⇨ memories and fantasies by ...

⇨ outward behaviour by ...

Analysing your script system like this could feel quite discouraging but by now you can see that it is important to understand how you are setting yourself up for anxiety so that you can do something about it.

The good news

It is possible to make changes to your whole script system by changing a single part of it, because each part influences the other parts. For example, if your thoughts change then your behaviour, internal experiences, memories and fantasies can also change. If your behaviour changes, then your thoughts, internal bodily experiences, memories and fantasies are free to change, too, and so on. If you work at changing one aspect, all the other parts of your system are also influenced in some way. In part III you will read about how to make changes to any of these areas.

It is time now to stop figuring out the 'whys' of exam anxiety and to move on to actually doing something about the un-wanted aspects of your borrowed and child patterns by using more of your adult insight. It is also time to make changes to your script system so that your adult insight can direct your script towards a happier and healthier life.

Chapter summary

This chapter contained 11 exercises to help you identify your borrowed and child patterns, as well as your script system and its maintenance.

⇨ Exercise 1 helped you understand your borrowed patterns in general.

⇨ Exercise 2 helped you understand your borrowed patterns in relation to exams.

⇨ Exercises 3 to 6 helped you understand your child patterns in general.

⇨ Exercise 7 helped you understand your child patterns in relation to exams.

⇨ Exercises 8 and 9 helped you understand how your borrowed and child patterns work together.

⇨ Exercise 10 helped you gauge your current level of adult insight in relation to exams.

⇨ Exercise 11 helped you understand the contents of your script system and how you are perpetuating it.

Part III of this book will help you change unwanted aspects of your patterns and script.

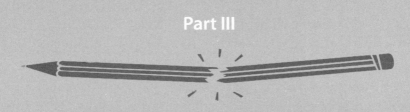

How do I get rid of my exam anxiety?

If we don't change the direction we're going, we're likely to end up where we are headed.

—Old Chinese proverb

Now that you understand your own borrowed and child patterns, as well as your script system, I am going to show you how you can change them so you can take your exams without anxiety and perform at your personal best. Your aim is to be at the top of the curve described in chapter 1.

There are four chapters in part III, each one dealing with an aspect of the script system.

⇨ Chapter 4 gives you tips on how to change your internal bodily experiences.

⇨ Chapter 5 gives you ideas on how you can change your behaviour.

⇨ Chapter 6 shows you how to change your beliefs and feelings so that they work for you, rather than against you.

⇨ Chapter 7 helps you deal with unwanted memories and focus on realistic and positive fantasies.

As we tackle each part of your script system, your first task will be to recognise what you are currently doing. Once you are aware of that you can make changes. Remember that each part influences the other parts, so the good news is that by working on one part you are also helping the others. This section contains exercises designed to help to change your script from being negative about exams to being positive about them. This section also contains helpful hints to maintain your newly formed and positive script system.

Chapter 4

How to change your internal bodily experiences

What goes on inside your body when you are stressed out in the lead-up to, just before, or even taking an exam? Does your body experience too much physical pressure at these times so you can't revise or perform at your personal best? In chapter 1 I explained that when we feel threatened by something our body gets into a state of high pressure, only returning to its normal equilibrium once the threat goes away. This equilibrium is often referred to as our 'resting state'. Exams, of course, won't go away that easily, and the anxiety reaction we have as a result of feeling threatened can play havoc on our bodies if it stays around too long. This happened to Grace, one of our case studies in chapter 1, and she got an itchy rash all over her body. You will soon learn how to control your anxiety reaction, but first it is important to understand exactly what this is doing to your body.

Some of the ideas in this chapter will suggest that you 'do' something but they are explained here, rather than in the next chapter on changing behaviour, because they are tips designed to specifically lower your level of internal pressure.

The effects of exams on your body

The following exercise will help you identify your body's response to exam anxiety. Once you have identified your body's physical early warning signs of anxiety you will be able to monitor yourself and act quickly when they begin to appear.

Exercise 12: understanding your physical early warning signs

Below is a list of common symptoms our bodies may experience if we are anxious for too long. Please remember that not all of these symptoms are necessarily caused by anxiety—some may have other underlying causes. If in doubt you must check your symptoms with a doctor.

Put a tick next to all the symptoms that apply to you.

- ☐ Raised heart rate
- ☐ Nausea
- ☐ Difficulty breathing
- ☐ Butterflies
- ☐ Breaking out in a rash
- ☐ Shallow or rapid breathing
- ☐ Feeling itchy

- ☐ High blood pressure
- ☐ Headaches
- ☐ Shivering
- ☐ Constipation
- ☐ Feeling hot/sweating
- ☐ Diarrhoea
- ☐ Dry mouth
- ☐ Feeling faint
- ☐ Salivation/frequent swallowing
- ☐ Acne
- ☐ Furrowed brow
- ☐ Chronic asthma
- ☐ Back problems
- ☐ Chronic allergies
- ☐ Proneness to illness
- ☐ Excessive tiredness/lethargy
- ☐ Tense/aching muscles
- ☐ Loss of/increased appetite
- ☐ Clenched jaw and/or fists
- ☐ Easily startled
- ☐ Other_____

The good news is that if these symptoms are being caused by prolonged anxiety then we can do something about them. When our body is presenting these symptoms it is because we are in a state of acute or chronic physical and psychological pressure, so if we learn to calm our body and reduce this pressure, the physical symptoms of anxiety will settle down.

As you now know, there are two types of anxious people: those who are anxious about lots of things, and those who are anxious about a specific thing. Remember chronically anxious Andy and exam-phobic Phom? Andy was anxious about several things that were going on in his life, but Phom was only anxious about exams. All of the suggestions for changing your internal bodily experiences are useful for both types of exam-anxious people. In fact, most of the suggestions can be incorporated into your life so that you can feel less anxious and stressed out in general.

Hint: incorporate some experiences into your life that reduce pressure

When people are asked what they do to relax they often answer in terms of playing sport, reading, playing music or some other sort of hobby. My question to you is more specific: what do you do, if anything, to lower the level of pressure in your body and calm yourself on the inside? This 'relaxing inside' is sometimes referred to as achieving the relaxation response.

If you are overly anxious the chances are that you don't incorporate calming techniques into your daily life. If this is the case, you will need to train your body to lower its pressure level. It's no good saying 'I know how to relax'; our brains may know what to do but our bodies won't achieve a calm state unless they're trained to do so. The training means practising some sort of physically relaxing or calming experience on a regular basis. You can start by practising a little each day. You may be thinking that you haven't got time to do this; however, if you can schedule some time for these activities into your life you will never regret it. You will gain a lifelong skill to help you through *any* stressful event, and you will probably be much healthier. You will have a feeling of calm inside your body, you won't feel threatened so easily, you will not experience physical symptoms of anxiety, and your anxious thoughts will become weaker or even disappear.

So what are the calming experiences I'm talking about? The most common ones are:

⇨ listening to a relaxation CD

⇨ meditating

⇨ doing yoga

⇨ getting a massage

⇨ having a relaxing bath

⇨ listening to calming music.

Different people like different activities so it is important to choose something that works for you—you may want to try out a range of different activities. Counsellors at your school, college or university can also teach you to relax and can probably lend you a relaxation CD if you ask. They'd also know what classes in yoga or meditation are available in your local area, and who the good massage practitioners are, as would your local community health centre or information centre.

Hint: study with Baroque music playing quietly in the background

Study with slow Baroque music (such as Pachelbel, Albinoni or Bach) playing very quietly in the background, perhaps on your computer or MP3 player. Before you roll your eyes, let me explain—slow Baroque music is said to be particularly calming. Its 60 beats a minute helps us to slow our heart rate and to reach a brain wave state that is helpful for concentration.

It therefore lowers our bodies' level of physiological pressure. If you study with this music playing quietly you can focus, concentrate and remember things much more easily. If you don't have any of this type of music, you can probably borrow a CD from your local library.

Hint: learn how to centre yourself (or calm yourself down 'on the spot')

Centering is another way of lowering your body's pressure level. It is included here as a separate hint because its use is slightly different to the activities listed above. While centering yourself will certainly lower your pressure level, it is also a skill that you can use at any time and whatever you are doing in order to calm yourself before a stressful situation. You can learn to centre yourself so that you can calm down before you revise, before you enter an exam room, when you feel stuck on a question, before an oral presentation or during an oral exam. This is a skill that can also be transferred to situations not related to exam anxiety, such as just before you make a difficult phone call or just before you enter a room full of strangers. Learning to centre yourself is a life skill. And the beauty of it is that, with practice, you can learn to centre yourself in just a few seconds—without anyone knowing you're doing so!

If you have ever listened to a relaxation CD, or meditated or practised yoga, then you will have learned that breath is very important when calming down. Slow, fairly deep, yet comfortable breathing relaxes the body. If you've ever seen anyone in a panic you will have noticed that they breathe quickly and shallowly.

Track 2 on the accompanying CD teaches you to centre yourself. After regular practice you will be able to do this when moving around and even when speaking, but first it is important to learn the technique in a comfortable position. Listen to this track as soon as you can and as often as you can until you can calm down on the spot relatively quickly. The next hint will help you monitor your progress.

Hint: practise lowering your pressure level after physical activity

Just as our pressure level goes up when we are anxious, so it does when we do some sort of physical activity. This type of activity gives us an opportunity to see if we can 'calm down' intentionally when our heart is beating fast and our breath is quick and shallow.

After you have exercised (you can run up a flight of stairs for the sake of this exercise), stand still and use the centering technique described earlier. Take your pulse as soon as you have finished the activity and then again after you have calmed down so you can see how your heart rate changes and practise using centering to lower it more quickly after exercise.

Hint: use the centering technique to improve your concentration and memory

We can't concentrate or remember things easily when we are anxious. Here is an additional method to help you revise that can be combined with the playing of Baroque music I suggested earlier.

Once you are sitting at your desk, but before you start revising, take a couple of minutes to centre yourself. If you start revising in a calm way you are more likely to stay focused and this will help your memory. You can also use this technique at the end of a revision session. Before you get up from your desk, centre yourself again and allow your mind to think back over what you just learned. You certainly won't remember everything, but you are likely to remember more if you stay calm. Remembering material from a revision session immediately after finishing also helps your long-term memory.

The reason I am suggesting you use the centering technique before and after a revision session is that when we feel relaxed our brain goes into a state called alpha brain wave state. This alpha state helps us to focus, concentrate and remember the task at hand. When we are not as relaxed our brain goes into the beta brain wave state and allows us to do things where we have to be aware of lots of things at once — for example, driving a car or having a logical conversation with another person. We use both brain wave states in our daily lives, but we only need the alpha brain wave state when we are trying to concentrate and remember.

Regular exercise helps you focus

Hopefully, you are already exercising regularly. Keep going with this regular exercise even if you are worried about time. If we suddenly stop exercising our body tends to react in ways that can interfere with our study — for example, we might feel sluggish. Exercise also raises endorphin levels in our body (endorphins are chemicals our body produces that make us happy), and that means that we feel psychologically, as well as physically, healthier. In other words, regular exercise will help you focus and also stress less.

Hint: listen to your body

Take time to listen to your body. Our bodies can tell us what they need but often we are too engrossed with outside events or just too busy to stop and listen to them. You now know that we experience certain symptoms when we let our anxiety get the better of us, so it is important to watch out for these warning signs and take note of them. Also, make sure you stretch when your body is aching. If you feel physically tense do an activity to lower your pressure level and give yourself the relaxation response. It is also important to sleep when you are tired, so if you have trouble sleeping the next hint will be important for you.

Hint: learn how to sleep well

When we are anxious our body and mind are often too wired to sleep well, if at all, and we can't revise or perform at our personal best when we are tired.

Learning to fall asleep is another great technique to have up your sleeve around exam time. Some tips are given in the box overleaf. In addition, have a CD player next to your bed (or use an MP3 player) and when you are ready to sleep put on track 4 on the CD, which is designed to help you fall asleep. It's been placed last so that you can fall asleep without another track waking you.

To wake up well, go outside first thing in the morning. This will shut down your body's production of night-time sleep hormones, called melatonin, and reset your brain for daytime activities. If you can do some exercise as soon as you wake this is even better, as exercise releases endorphins into your body and gives you energy to study or revise.

How to get a good night's sleep

- Don't get too hot or cold. Have layers on your bed that you can adjust during the night.

- Turn your mobile off. Don't use your phone as an alarm if, as a result, you can hear a call coming through.

- Turn off any other electronic equipment that may make noise during the night.

- Don't eat late at night.

- Don't have any caffeine or alcohol before bed. Alcohol and any other non-prescription drugs should be avoided altogether in the lead-up to your exams.

- Keep regular sleeping hours, if possible. Decide on your bed time and rising time in the lead-up to exams and stick to these times.

- Some people like to write a journal of the day before they sleep — it helps them 'finish' the day.

- Keep a sheet of paper next to your bed and jot down anything you think of after lying down and that you want to remember in the morning. That way you can forget about it for the time being.

- Turn your clock to the wall. Looking at the time will only make you anxious.

- Have a firm and comfortable bed. If necessary, put some slats under the mattress.

- Make sure the room is dark.

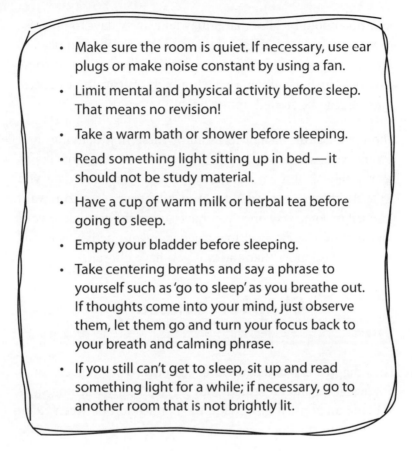

- Make sure the room is quiet. If necessary, use ear plugs or make noise constant by using a fan.
- Limit mental and physical activity before sleep. That means no revision!
- Take a warm bath or shower before sleeping.
- Read something light sitting up in bed — it should not be study material.
- Have a cup of warm milk or herbal tea before going to sleep.
- Empty your bladder before sleeping.
- Take centering breaths and say a phrase to yourself such as 'go to sleep' as you breathe out. If thoughts come into your mind, just observe them, let them go and turn your focus back to your breath and calming phrase.
- If you still can't get to sleep, sit up and read something light for a while; if necessary, go to another room that is not brightly lit.

Exercise 13: your promise to yourself

By now you should have lots of ideas to help your body calm down. Go back over these now and pick out two activities you are going to do on a regular basis to help you stay calm. I strongly suggest that one of these is learning how to centre yourself. Write these activities in your notebook.

Now I want you to make a contract with yourself to do whatever it is you have written down on a regular basis. When the time comes, write the dates that you started your activities in your notebook. I realise that it may take a few days to organise an activity you have chosen if it is one that means you need to attend a class—for example, yoga or meditation—but some activities, such as taking a relaxing bath or learning to centre yourself, can be started immediately.

Allow your adult insight to monitor these new activities and remind you when you forget to do them. You might like to keep track of how you are going by marking the date you do these things on a calendar. You might also like to reward yourself in some way once you have successfully stuck to your contract for a week. Feel free to change your activities at any time, or to do more than the two you have chosen.

Chapter summary

This chapter explained ways of lowering your anxiety on a physical level and identified your physical early warning signs of being anxious. It also made the connection between exam revision and staying calm.

In this chapter you have learned that:

⇨ if we learn to stay calm our physical symptoms of anxiety will disappear

⇨ incorporating calming experiences into our daily lives lowers our resting state of pressure and gives us the relaxation response. These experiences need to be done regularly to work

⇨ listening to Baroque music while revising helps lower pressure and improve concentration and memory

⇨ centering helps us calm down on the spot and is a useful technique to use while studying for an exam, when thinking about an exam and when taking an exam, as well as for non-exam-related situations

⇨ centering ourselves after physical activity is a means of practising to calm down

⇨ centering ourselves before and after revision helps us concentrate and remember things more easily

⇨ getting enough sleep is very important.

In this chapter you also made a promise to yourself to participate in at least two relaxing activities regularly and monitor your progress towards being free from exam anxiety.

Chapter 5

How to change your behaviour

The word 'behaviour' refers to anything we do that can be observed by another person. Although you were asked to 'do' things in the last chapter, they were specifically related to your physical responses to anxiety. In this chapter you will be doing other things to change your behaviour that will also help lower your anxiety as exams approach.

The effects of exams on your behaviour

The following exercises will help you identify and change your behavioural responses to exam anxiety. Once you have done this you will be able to monitor yourself and, if necessary, seek help to change negative behaviour when it presents itself.

Exercise 14: understanding your behavioural early warning signs

Your first job is to think about what *you* do when you start to get anxious about exams. Looking back at our earlier case studies, Sol avoided putting himself in situations where his perceived stupidity would show, Annie cried, and Ross drank heavily. Other examples of behavioural early warning signs are finding excuses not to study, being irritable or forgetful, being unable to sleep, wasting time on the computer or phone, checking things that are not necessary to check, or changes in appetite. There are plenty of other ways that we can behave when we get anxious, too.

How do you behave when you start to get anxious about exams? Write your observations down in your notebook.

Asking for help and support

It goes without saying really, but to be able to take an exam successfully you need to understand the subject matter. Do you really understand it or are there some parts of your subjects that aren't clear? If so, it is extremely important that you ask your teacher, lecturer or tutor for some academic help. Don't be shy. If it is too hard to speak to them after a lecture, or if your lecture notes are delivered electronically, try emailing them.

Students are often too scared to ask for help and this anxiety can be caused by one or more problems. Some students say they are ashamed they need help, particularly if they haven't been turning up to class. For others, they are just plain scared of their teacher. Many students rarely—if ever—ask for help.

If you are a part-time or off-campus student (or both), you may find it too difficult to speak to your teacher face-to-face, but you can email them and ask to set up a time to talk by phone. Don't let your borrowed patterns (for example, 'I should know the answer') or your child patterns ('If I ask, the teacher will get angry') get in the way.

Apart from academic help, it is also important to set up an emotional support system, particularly if you are very anxious about your exams. Exercise 15 will help you understand why you find it hard to ask for help when you need it.

We are now going to look at more positive ways to behave so that you can study and take your exam without anxiety.

Exercise 15: understanding why you struggle to ask for help

If you are one of those students who don't ask for help, why don't you? What's in your borrowed or child patterns that stops you from doing so? If it were just up to your adult insight you wouldn't hesitate to ask for help—there is something you are telling yourself that stops you. This will be a belief that you have, which is really just another part of your script system. Let's find out what this belief is now, because it is very important to be able to ask for help when you need it in order to reduce your anxiety around exams.

Write a couple of sentences in your notebook about why you find it so hard to ask for help, keeping in mind they will be a reflection of either your borrowed or child patterns, or both.

When you next want to ask for help, go to your teacher or lecturer, armed with your adult insight, and ask. I know this may sound hard, but once you have asked once or twice it will get easier. Remind yourself that it is just an old pattern getting in the way. We will work more on how to change your beliefs and feelings in chapter 6 and, if necessary, you can look deeper into what is stopping you from asking for help with the exercises in that chapter. In the meantime, remind yourself that your teachers or lecturers are paid to teach you—it's part of their job description.

It could also be useful to ask another student for some help —someone who is studying the same subject, or perhaps someone who did well in the subject in a previous year. If your subject has an electronic message board or blog then use it.

Hint: get emotional support

You also need to set up a good emotional support system for yourself at exam time. You need to find people who have good nurturing instincts and these people need to understand that you are confronting your anxiety about exams. It is important that you can trust them. It is probably good to have at least two people who can provide you with this support, as one or more of them may not always be available to support you, or perhaps they each offer a different type of support.

Your supporters need to be able to listen, give helpful advice and be there for you—at least on the end of a phone line or on the internet. You might like to tell them things about how your study is going, what problems you are having, how you are feeling, and how your body is coping with the stress. You may even like to ask them for a head massage or back rub, or you could ask them to come out and 'play' with you when you want to get into some positive child patterns.

Remember that you can always pay these people back in some way after your exams; perhaps by helping them in some way or by buying them a small gift. However, when they see you confronting your anxiety and dealing with it successfully, this may be all the reward they need.

Who will you choose to be on your support team? Write their names in your notebook, as well as the dates you asked them to help you.

Hint: set up a peer study group

Students often find that their anxiety is lowered if they study a subject with other students. You will need to use your adult insight to pick suitable people. These people don't have to be your friends, as friends often get into fun child patterns too easily and take energy away from the purpose of your meeting, which is to revise together and go over difficult material. Also, the people you choose shouldn't be those who will take up too much group time because they are too needy for help—you need both givers and takers in a study group.

The idea of a study group is to find a couple of other students (three students to a group is a good number) and arrange to meet regularly to revise. You should all be committed to the task and not find excuses to not turn up. If it is too hard to meet face-to-face you can set up a chat room and meet electronically. You should all spend roughly the same amount of time talking in the meeting and contribute evenly to discussion. Remember: the idea is peer support. Most importantly, you must use your adult insight while the group is focused on studying, unless you choose to borrow a creative child pattern to make studying more interesting.

Hint: find out what to do if you get stuck on a question in the exam

It is not only the subject matter where you may need some help; it is also important to make sure you understand what to do if you get stuck on an exam question. If this happens you may get anxious during the exam, which may in turn affect your performance. How you deal with this will depend on the type of exam you are doing. If it is a written question it is relatively easy to leave a gap and return to the question if you have time. But what if you get stuck on a calculation and the answer is needed for another question? This is where you should ask your teacher or lecturer for advice. Some teachers will suggest you guess the answer in order to move on to the next question. Others might suggest that you write out how you would get the answer in the next question if you hadn't got stuck on the first. Some teachers will suggest doing both, or may have a completely different idea. And what if you get stuck in an oral exam? Again, your teacher or lecturer will tell you how best to deal with this situation. It is important you ask *before* an exam, so that you know what to do if the situation arises.

Planning and managing your time

In this section on planning and managing your time we will cover three areas: the lead-up to an exam, single study sessions (including the use of half-hour sessions), and coping with a large crisis or event in your life.

Organise your time in the lead-up to an exam

Managing your time well during your revision weeks is a must. Good time management goes a long way towards lowering your anxiety level. If you know you are on track with your revision you will feel more relaxed and your concentration will improve, too.

How well do you manage your time now? Exercise 16 will help you decide.

Exercise 16: how well do you currently manage your time?

Thinking back to your last exam, how would you rate yourself on a scale of 0 to 10, with 0 being totally disorganised in the area of revision scheduling and 10 being completely organised?

If you thought you were fairly well organised here is another scale for you. On a scale of 0 to 10, with 0 being completely unable to stick to your revision schedule and 10 being totally on track in this regard, how would you rate yourself?

Are you happy with your revision planning? Even if you are, you may still learn some new ideas in this section. I am a great believer in the 'try it and see' approach, rather than the 'if it ain't broke, don't fix it' tactic.

Hint: set realistic goals and achieve them

This hint relates to goals spread over six weeks or more, and also very short-term goals, even as short as half an hour. Your goals must not only be possible, they must also be realistic—if you do more than you set out to do, well and good, but you must at the very least reach the goals you set for yourself. If you have an achievable goal to work towards you will be more motivated, concentrate better and have a lower anxiety level. Rewards, however small, for reaching your goals will help, too.

Compare the case studies of Sarah and Brett.

Sarah

Sarah is a first-year student at university. She really enjoys university life, particularly her social life. She attends classes and gets her assignments done on time, but is finding it very hard to revise for exams—classes and assignments have timetables and deadlines, but the only deadline for revision is the exam itself.

Exams are about four weeks away and Sarah keeps telling herself that she 'should' revise but always finds a reason for not staying at her desk. She goes out with friends when she should be revising, and when she does sit at her desk she wishes she were out with her friends. She starts a revision session without a clear idea of what she is going to revise or for how long—she has no goals so if she gets a phone call inviting her out, she goes. After all, the deadline of exams is quite a long way away.

As the exams get closer Sarah starts to feel anxious. Will she ever know enough to pass? She is secretly frustrated with her behaviour and feels depressed about letting herself down. This is a familiar feeling. Sarah has always felt the need to be liked and has often put this need above her desire to study and be successful. Her adult insight has not pulled her child pattern of needing to be liked into line yet.

Brett, on the other hand, tackles his revision differently.

Brett

Brett is a friend of Sarah's and is doing the same course at university. He goes to classes and meets the deadlines for his assignments, and he also likes going out and being sociable — just like Sarah.

Brett knows he has to revise for his exams and that if he sets goals and targets for his revision he will know enough to pass, and pass well, by the time the exams arrive. He works to a revision timetable and also has clear goals for his revision sessions, which he usually meets. He also allows himself time to go out and be sociable, and rewards himself in small ways, too, like watching a favourite TV show after a revision session. His adult insight is in charge and he is focused on his exams, knowing he can go out to have fun and be social far more often once his exams are over. He is not frustrated, anxious or depressed — he is motivated to succeed.

The point is that if you set reachable goals and regularly fulfil them, your attitude towards exams will spiral upwards and make you feel motivated. You will feel good about yourself and more energised. If, however, you set goals and rarely fulfil them, then you will spiral downwards and end up feeling unmotivated and even depressed. Don't forget to treat yourself from time to time when you reach one of your goals.

Hint: set a realistic revision timetable

Setting and sticking to a realistic revision schedule lowers anxiety and helps you get through the weeks leading up to an exam period. The following exercise will help you set a revision timetable for your own situation.

Exercise 17: how to make a revision timetable

In this exercise you are going to set up your own revision timetable for your exams.

To start, take two A4 pieces of paper or set up two documents on your computer. Divide the first page into the number of subjects you are studying by making columns—for example, if you are studying three subjects divide your paper into three columns. Make sure you have a column for each subject, even if you don't have an exam for each one, as you are probably still writing or doing assignments.

At the top of each column put the title of the subject. Under each title write down all the topics within that subject that you will need to know for the exam. Also, write down any assignments still due for that subject. Once you have listed all the topics you then need to decide if you are going to revise for all of them—this will depend on how much choice of questions you will have in the exam. If there is going to be a wide range of question options then you *may* be able to take some risks and not study each topic, but you must be very confident that you can disregard something before doing so. If the choice is narrow or no choice is given, then you will have to revise for every topic.

Now divide the second piece of paper into squares corresponding to the number of weeks you have left before the exam—for example, if you have six weeks left, divide your paper into six squares. Label each square with the date of the start of that week. Then in each square write any assignments due that week and the topics to be revised. You will end up with a list of topics and assignments due for each week and so you will now have weekly goals, which you must stick to. Before you start your timetable, read the tips listed below.

⇨ If your assignments are going to take more than
a week to complete then make sure you list your
assignment work under each appropriate week.

⇨ Make sure you revise for each subject, each week,
until you get close to the exam period, when you will
probably want to focus only on the closest exam.

⇨ Leave time to 're-revise' for each topic. The more you
go over material, the easier it will be to remember.

⇨ Leave some 'just in case' time for each topic—just
in case you come down with a cold or get an
unexpected invitation to something.

⇨ Make sure that your goals for each week are
manageable so you don't get anxious. If it looks like
you can't possibly revise what you have listed then
you will have to decide whether or not to leave a
topic out or else revise them all less thoroughly.

⇨ Reward yourself when you reach your goals.

Planning your revision lowers your anxiety level and we revise more easily if we are less anxious. Allow your adult insight to take over and plan your revision with reachable goals—if you stick to the plan you will know you've done enough to pass.

Planning a study session

For starters, it is worth emphasising the importance of having a study space of your own, however small, where you don't have to move your books so that other people can use the space—the end of the kitchen table is not a good idea. It's better to set up a small table just for you somewhere else, even if it's in a nook. Having a space of your own lowers your level of anxiety.

The idea of setting achievable goals and fulfilling them applies to revision sessions, too, but there is a bit more to planning a revision session than simply setting a goal—we have to warm up to study and get our bottom on the seat! Did you know that most people can only fully concentrate for about 20 minutes at a time? This is not to say that your study sessions should only be 20 minutes long—if you include warm-up and wind-down time, a study session can last for much longer, and warm-up time can start well before you even get to your desk.

Have a look at the graph in figure 5.1, which shows the concentration curve. The curve shows that you need to warm up before you can fully concentrate and that you should wind down after a period of full concentration. Once you reach a point in your wind-down where sitting at your desk is not a productive thing to do, it is time for a break—however small—and then you will be ready to start the curve again. If your break was a small one you won't need as much time to warm up, particularly if you are continuing the same topic.

Figure 5.1: concentration curve

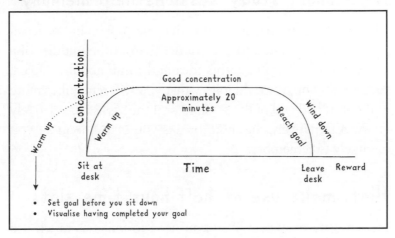

Hint: warm up before you sit down

You can start to warm up before you even put your bottom on the seat and this is a good thing to do. In the minutes before you sit down, decide what you are going to revise and visualise yourself having done so. You can even do this while doing other things, such us cleaning up after a meal, exercising or walking home from school.

Hint: centre yourself before and after a revision session

After you have sat down at your desk and just before you start revising, take time to centre yourself. By doing this you will lower any anxiety you have and also increase your ability to concentrate. Don't forget to centre yourself again at the end of your study session, before recalling as much as you can of the material you just revised.

Hint: short study sessions help memory

There is a theory that maintains that the probability of recall is higher at the start and end, rather than in the middle, of a study session. If we take this idea and think about a typical revision session, it would follow that you will remember more at the start and end of the session, or if the session is relatively short. Alternatively, the more breaks you take, the more you are likely to remember.

Hint: make use of half-hour time slots

Students are busy people so you need to make as much use of your time as you can. You may have half an hour on public transport, before a class, or perhaps while waiting for someone. Use this time. It soon adds up.

Half-hour goals are useful for at least four things:

⇨ if you are particularly anxious then half-hour goals are less overwhelming

⇨ if you are learning 'by heart' — research shows that it is best to do this for only short periods at a time

⇨ if you are going over any summaries or memory joggers that you have made of a topic

⇨ if you are a procrastinator, half-hour goals are usually a good way to get you going.

As you can see, there are some very useful things you can do with just half an hour, so never tell yourself it's not enough time.

Revising while coping with a crisis or major event in your life

Unfortunately, everybody's lives have times of crisis, or big events at the 'wrong' time. These events may even be pleasurable—for example, your sister may decide to get married around the time of your exams. Whatever the situation, you have to keep on revising even though you have a lot going on, both physically and emotionally.

How do you keep revising when something major is going on in your life? The answer to this question involves goals again, but in a different way. There is a useful technique called 'time out for worry' and it can also be used when you need to do lots of things for an upcoming pleasurable occasion, such as a wedding. We will stick with a crisis for the sake of explanation.

Paul came to the university's counselling service just a few weeks before his exams to seek help. We will use his situation to illustrate the concept of 'time out for worry'.

Paul

Paul is a final-year accounting student at university. A few days before he saw the counsellor, his father was diagnosed with a terminal illness and told that his life expectancy was very short. Paul's family is very close and they all, particularly his father, wanted Paul to go ahead and take his exams. Because these were Paul's final exams at university, he had secured a job and was

Paul (cont'd)

due to start as soon as his results came through — he had to pass in order to work as an accountant.

His father's wish was that Paul take his exams and secure the job. Paul was feeling torn. He wanted to spend more time with his dying father but he also wanted to take his exams so he could start to earn good money as soon as possible, which would help his family. When Paul came to the counselling service, apart from focusing on his grief, the counsellor also had to focus on helping him revise. She asked him to pick a couple of hours in the day that weren't immediately before bed and were also not when he felt best able to revise. Paul said late afternoon was a good time and so this became his 'time out for worry'. We can't worry and study at the same time, but we can do so at different times.

The counsellor asked Paul to dedicate a couple of hours at the same time each day to do things to help his grief, such as visiting his father or writing his feelings in a journal — this was his time for grief. When he was freshest, that was his time to revise. This technique is not as silly as it may sound. If we know we have time to deal with a crisis we are more able to get on with things like revising. Of course, it is important that Paul also uses all the other goal-setting techniques to help him. Short-term goals would be particularly helpful if he found his concentration span was short. In times of grief our child patterns tend to play a major role in our script system and we need to make sure we look after ourselves. Paul needed to find time to focus on exams so he didn't get anxious.

We tend to use this technique a bit unknowingly, too. How many times have you heard someone say, 'When I'm at work I can just forget about it, but when I'm at home I worry a lot'? We can compartmentalise our lives when we need to.

Active learning helps to lower anxiety

An active learner is a student who *does* something other than reading and trying to remember in order to revise. A passive learner is someone who stares at the information they are trying to remember, hoping it will just be absorbed by their memory in some unexplained way—it won't! We can't remember unless we actively engage in the process of learning.

Unless we give ourselves permission to study differently, we tend to study in the way we were taught by our schoolteachers. If this is the case, borrowed patterns are definitely at work. Today teachers seem to encourage active learning but if you are an older student, or a student who went to school in a different culture, you may have been encouraged to learn passively by just repeating what the teachers said, rather than thinking things through for yourself. If you were encouraged to learn passively then you may also revise passively, which may in turn increase your anxiety. If you are a passive learner the following hint is an important one for you.

Hint: vary the way you revise

The thing you have to do to help you revise is to recall information using as many and as varied ways as possible.

For example, with any topic you could:

⇨ read about it

⇨ think about it

⇨ draw a diagram of it

⇨ ask questions about it

⇨ explain it to someone else (or yourself in a mirror or the dog—it's the speaking out loud that is important)

⇨ answer a past exam question on it (this also means you can make sure that your hand can write legibly for the required length of time)

⇨ summarise it (carry this around to test yourself when you have a few minutes)

⇨ be interviewed about it

⇨ study it in a group

⇨ role-play being the teacher.

The ideas that require you to speak out loud are really important because you have to go from thinking to speaking, which means you will definitely find out what you don't know about a subject. Did you know that we think at up to 60 000 words a minute but we only speak at approximately 180 words a minute? It's easy to gloss over ideas when you are thinking about them but not so easy when you are speaking out loud.

If your exam is an oral exam you will need to practise speaking out loud a lot. You might like to make up possible exam questions and answer them out loud as well—to someone or just to yourself. If you speak to someone you get the added advantage of asking them to stop you and ask questions if they don't understand.

Hint: recall, recall, recall

However you decide to revise, make sure you recall, recall, recall, in order to remember. Here are some statistics to put this hint into perspective:

⇨ we lose up to 40 per cent of what we read if we don't recall the information within two minutes

⇨ we lose up to 60 per cent of what we read if we don't recall the information within two hours

⇨ we lose up to 80 per cent of information if we don't recall it for a month

⇨ students remember more if they recall their lectures each evening, before going on to revise or study specific information.

Familiarise yourself with exam details

Some people say that anxiety is 'fear of the unknown', so make the unknown known, as far as you can with regards to your exams. It is important to obtain as much information as you can about your exam in the weeks leading up to it. Following are some tips on the type of information you should be asking for.

• Make sure you get all the necessary information about the venue of the exam as soon as it's available. Try to get into the venue beforehand if it is unfamiliar and orient yourself. This is especially important if you are giving an oral presentation.

• Make sure you have all the details about the exam itself. Find out how long it is, what the

Familiarise yourself with exam details *(cont'd)*

format of the questions is and what each question is worth in terms of marks.

- Find out how much choice of questions there is in the exam. If there is a lot of choice you may choose not to revise every aspect of the subject matter, but if there is little or no choice, you can't afford to gamble on your revision.

- Find out about what you will need for the exam in terms of equipment — for example, pens, compasses, calculators and rulers — and make sure you take them with you.

- If you are taking an oral exam make sure you know how many people are on the exam panel and, if possible, who they are. Do some research on them to help you understand their interest in sitting on your exam panel.

- If you are doing a multiple-choice exam check to see if marks are deducted for wrong answers. Guessing becomes a completely different issue if this is the case.

Look after yourself

It may be stating the obvious to say that you need to take care of yourself as exams are approaching, but your adult insight will need to overcome any borrowed or child patterns you don't want to use, paying particular attention to any unhealthy pressure you put on yourself around exam time. You read about several ways to look after yourself in the previous chapter and here are some more to keep you going at exam time.

⇨ Make sure you schedule time for leisure and pleasure.

⇨ Go out with non-student friends so you're not reminded of study.

⇨ Don't diet. Dieters are more forgetful because so much of their memory is taken up with thoughts of food.

⇨ Show your true emotions to people you trust, or at least let them out in private. Bottled up emotions cause psychological stress. Some people find it useful to keep a journal and write their emotions out.

⇨ Make sure you have a few belly laughs every day. This raises endorphin levels and reduces anxiety.

Exercise 18: your promise to yourself

You have now recognised your early behavioural warning signs and have been given some hints on how to change your behaviour so that it works *for* you rather than *against* you. Changing your behaviour in a large-scale way is usually too hard to do all at once, so take it slow. I want you to pick out three ideas from the hints given that you feel would really help you at this point in time. Write them in your notebook.

Now I want you to make another contract with yourself to do whatever it is that you have written down. It might be a one-off activity—for example, finding out some details about the exam, or it might be something you do on a regular basis, such as telling people how you are going. Allow your adult insight to monitor these new behaviours and pull you back into line you when you forget. You may like to reward yourself when you have spent a week successfully completing your contract! When you feel ready you can start practising other new behaviours.

Chapter summary

This chapter explained ways of lowering your anxiety by changing your behaviour.

Firstly, you identified your behavioural early warning signs of anxiety. The chapter then covered the following areas to help lower your anxiety:

⇨ asking for academic assistance when necessary

⇨ setting up a peer study group

⇨ getting emotional support

⇨ planning your revision schedule

⇨ planning a study session

⇨ setting reasonable goals and achieving them

⇨ revising actively

⇨ revising with a large crisis or event going on in your life

⇨ familiarising yourself with exam details

⇨ finding out what to do if you get stuck on an exam question

⇨ taking care of yourself.

You also made a promise to yourself to follow at least three of the hints in this chapter.

Chapter 6

How to change your beliefs and feelings

When we have negative thoughts and feelings about ourselves, others and the world in general we can get very anxious. Exam-anxious students usually have negative thoughts and feelings about exams. These thoughts and feelings affect our behaviour and what is going on inside our bodies, and also causes exam-anxious students to remember exams with anxiety.

The effects of beliefs and feelings on your exams

We need to take one last look at the negative beliefs and feelings that have contributed to your exam anxiety. Once we have drawn all these together we can work at getting rid of them.

Exercise 19: bringing your 'negativity' together

Look back at exercise 2 in chapter 3 and write any borrowed patterns that you want to eliminate or change in your notebook. You may want to add to them or change them in some way at this point.

Now look back at exercises 7, 8 and 9 in chapter 3 and write any child patterns that you want to eliminate or change in your notebook. Again, you may want to alter them in some way.

Finally, look back at the beliefs and feelings you wrote down in exercise 11 in chapter 3 in relation to the areas of exams, study, success, education and careers, and write them in your notebook under the relevant categories of 'me', 'others' and 'the world'. Feel free to add any more beliefs and feelings.

Now that you have reminded yourself of your old beliefs and feelings, the remaining exercises in this chapter will help you to change any negative statements you have written down about your patterns and script into more productive and positive statements.

Exercise 20: creating a new influential person in your head

We have to accept the people who gave us our borrowed and child patterns for who they were, or are. We can't go back and change the influence that these people have had on our lives, but we can create a new and positive influential person in our head. This positive influence can coexist with the more negative influences and broaden our repertoire of borrowed patterns to include far more positive messages, which our adult insight can borrow when necessary. You can influence your thoughts and feelings and let these new patterns exist inside your mind, as well as the negative influences you have taken on board. Over time you will only want to pay attention to the positive ones.

What would you like to tell yourself that will influence you about exams? You may like to choose messages from real or imagined people, or perhaps from a character in a book or film. Firstly, let's look at what Annie might choose.

Annie may tell herself that exams are not life threatening; they are only a small chapter in one's life, and perhaps students should make informed decisions about their career goals and not just follow their parents' advice.

What new messages would you like to influence *you*? Write them in your notebook.

If you are having trouble writing down your new influential messages (and even if you're not), think about what you would like to say about exams and related areas to a child that *you* might have or care for, either now or in the future. Write this down in your notebook.

Hint: remind yourself of your new influential messages

Write each influential message on a separate piece of paper and put one message on your desk where you can see it easily, or perhaps put it as an electronic reminder on your computer screen. Change the message each day and do this until you really do believe them.

Exercise 21: writing a letter to the child in you

Sometimes students find it helpful to solidify their new influential messages by writing a letter to the child part of themselves. Keep your letter somewhere you can re-read it from time to time, especially when you are starting to feel anxious. Here is an example of Annie's letter to help you.

> *Dear little Annie,*
>
> *Whatever you choose to do in life you will have my love and support. Although your life will be full of challenges, it is important to look after yourself in the best way that you can. I wish you a happy and fulfilling life full of fun, good health and happiness. I will always be there to look out for you.*
>
> *Love from Big Annie*

Ross, on the other hand, might write something like this.

> *Hi Ross,*
>
> *Being an 'academic child' is not the only way to be, or even necessarily the best way to be. Just give things your best shot and make sure you enjoy your life. You are not a 'loser', you are just different from your brother and sister, and there is nothing wrong with being different. In fact, being different can lead to many fantastic opportunities. Follow your dreams and have a wonderful life. I will always be here to lend a hand if things get rough.*
>
> *Love Big Ross*

Write your letter in your notebook.

Challenge your stressful thoughts

One way of changing your beliefs and feelings is to use your adult insight to challenge your thoughts and find more useful ones to take their place so that more appropriate feelings follow.

Below are some examples of typical thoughts that can make a student feel anxious about exams, ways of challenging these thoughts, and more useful thoughts to replace them.

Example 1

Negative thought: If I ask for help, people will think I am stupid.

Challenge: Are you absolutely sure people will think you are stupid? How do you know? They would probably be pleased that you are asking for their help as it shows that you think they know. Most people don't mind helping others. Teachers get paid to help. Even if someone did think you were stupid, so what? Your life isn't going to fall apart just because one person thinks you are stupid.

Useful thoughts: I need to understand this subject in order to pass the exam. If this means asking for help, that's okay. I owe it to myself.

Example 2

Negative thought: I will go blank in the exam because I did once before.

Challenge: Just because it happened before, does this mean it will definitely happen again? What evidence do you have that this will be the case?

113

Challenge your stressful thoughts (cont'd)

What will happen if you do go blank? Do you know what to do when this happens?

Useful thoughts: I have learned how to centre myself and keep calm and I am able to put this skill into action when I need to. There's no reason for me to go blank because I can control my anxiety.

Example 3

Negative thought: My parents or friends will be very disappointed if I fail.

Challenge: How sure are you about this and what evidence do you have that they'll react badly? Why is it so important that you keep these people happy? What will happen if they are disappointed? Do they measure you by what you achieve or who you are? Will your whole world fall apart if you do disappoint them?

Useful thoughts: My parents or friends may or may not be disappointed if I fail. If they are disappointed they will manage and cope. I can't control how they feel.

Exercise 22: challenging your negative thoughts

Now put your adult insight to work and do the same for your own negative thoughts about exams. In your notebook, explore and challenge at least three negative thoughts.

You may be thinking that it's one thing to create useful thoughts but another to really believe them. However, now that your adult insight has identified these new thoughts it can remind you of them each time it catches you thinking the old ones.

Hint: ways to remind yourself of your more useful thoughts

⇨ Say your new thoughts out loud, perhaps as you look in a mirror.

⇨ Say the new thoughts to people you trust.

⇨ Bring your thoughts into conversation when you can.

⇨ Write your new thoughts on a piece of paper or on your computer and leave them where you look regularly—for example, on your computer desktop or on the fridge.

⇨ Try a technique called 'thought stopping'. Every time you catch yourself having a negative thought, see a flashing red light saying 'stop' in front of you and then say your useful thought, preferably out loud.

⇨ Notice how differently you are feeling whenever your thoughts change and enjoy it.

Exercise 23: role-play telling your influential people how you are going to think, feel and behave differently towards exams

Firstly, read through the instructions for this entire exercise, including the examples. You may find this exercise difficult so take your time.

Exercise 8 in chapter 3 asked you to tell three people who had a strong influence over you how you were thinking and feeling about your forthcoming exam. That exercise was to help you understand your child patterns. In this exercise we are going to return to these people, but this time we will take the exercise further by telling them how things are going to be different now. I want you to tell them how you are going to think, feel and behave differently towards exams. Use the ideas you developed in the previous three exercises — for example, use exercise 20 to tell them about the new influential 'person' in your head and how this person (you!) is nurturing you through your exams. Or, using exercise 21, tell them what you wrote in your letter to your child self.

This exercise might make you feel uncomfortable, and if so, you must stop and ground yourself when your feelings become overwhelming. If you can complete the exercise you will have made a big shift in your beliefs and feelings and successfully confronted the influential people who gave you your borrowed patterns.

Set up two chairs facing each other in a room, and sit in one of them. Be sure to centre yourself before you start. When you are ready, imagine one of your influential people sitting in the other chair and tell them what you think and how you feel about the patterns that you borrowed from them. Now, tell them how you are going to think, feel and behave differently towards your exams.

You can take this exercise one step further if you like. When you have finished telling your influential person everything you have to say, sit in the other chair and as that other person reply to what you have just said. This is a big ask, and you may be surprised by what you have to say as this person. Finally,

116

go back and be yourself again and give a final reply. When you have finished, take a deep breath, stand up and reorient yourself to your current world by grounding yourself again.

Eventually, I would like you to have a dialogue with all three of your influential people so you may like to do this exercise over a couple of days. Always remember to centre yourself first, to ground yourself if you need to stop during the exercise, and to ground yourself at the end of each dialogue.

Below is a brief example of Annie's dialogue to help you.

> **Annie:** Hi Dad. I'm glad you're sitting here because I want to tell you my news. I've been working on my exam anxiety and I've realised just how much you influenced me to study hard, get a good job and be the best at that job. Well, I've decided that I do want to study hard, but not at the expense of my health and wellbeing. I want to become an architect, but it's very hard to get into the course. If I do miss out, I have another option to fall back on. I don't feel the need to be a top architect, but if that does happen it would be a great bonus. Right now I'm going to take care of myself while I'm studying, and just wait and see what happens next.

> **Dad:** Well, Annie, you know you have to study very hard. It's no good being just any old architect—if you want to do well in that profession you need to be one of the best. If you study hard enough you could get to the top. I'd be so proud of you.

> **Annie:** I'm sad that you still feel I need to make it to the top. I may be good at what I do if I become an architect, or I may find that it just doesn't suit me. I can't see into the future. I'm also sad that you can only be proud of

me if I get to the top of a profession. I'd like you to be proud of me for doing my best, wherever that may lead I can't make you be proud of me, but I will manage and cope whether you're proud of me or not.

Ross's dialogue might go something like this:

Ross: Hi Joe. Believe it or not I've been to see a counsellor recently. I'm fed up with stacking shelves, so I'm going to go back to college to try a different course—I want to become a graphic artist! This time it is going to be different, though. The counsellor is helping me to come to terms with the fact that I'm different from you. I'm not as academic, but this certainly doesn't make me a 'loser'. There is an artistic part of me that I never knew about and I'm going to develop it. The counsellor is also helping me with my anxiety over exams. I didn't want to see a counsellor before because I thought people would think I was stupid if I needed help, but now I think differently. I know it's not 'stupid' to seek help—it's 'stupid' not to!

Joe: Fantastic! That's all great news. To be honest I always thought that everyone was very hard on you but I wasn't able to stand up and defend you back then. I'm sorry that I wasn't strong enough to do that. I actually found it hard at university. It wasn't easy for me and I failed a couple of courses along the way, not that I spent a lot of time talking about that!

Ross: You were scared of being called a loser, too! We can be so hard on ourselves, can't we? And we're the only ones that lose out. We do it to ourselves. That's all changing for me though!

Of course, you are only confronting these people in a role-play exercise. What would happen if you actually met up with them? You have options if this happens and you must use your adult insight to decide how to handle the situation. You may decide to talk to them in reality, and this conversation may or may not go quite like it did in your role-play. Or you may decide to protect yourself by hearing what they have to say but not responding to them, knowing that you are solid in your new beliefs and this is what counts. The choice is yours.

We have now explored how to change three of the four parts of your script system. The next chapter helps you deal with the final part, your negative memories and fantasies.

Chapter summary

This chapter explained ways of reducing your anxiety by changing your beliefs and feelings.

Firstly, you identified the negative beliefs and feelings about exams that you discovered by doing the exercises in chapter 3. The chapter also covered the following areas to help you change these beliefs and feelings:

⇨ you created a new and positive influential person in your head

⇨ you wrote a letter to the child in you to solidify your new messages to yourself

⇨ you learned how to challenge your negative thoughts

⇨ you learned ways of reminding yourself of your more useful thoughts

⇨ you role-played conversations between yourself and the people that instilled your negative beliefs and feelings, with the aim of solidifying your new ones.

Chapter 7

How to change your memories and fantasies

In this chapter you will be exploring your memories and fantasies and how they contribute to your exam anxiety. To recap, memories are thoughts that we have when we think about something that actually happened in the past, while fantasies are thoughts that we have when we think about what could have happened in the past or what could happen in the future.

Reinforcing memories and fantasies is the last of the four areas of the script system to be explored. When we dwell on negative past events or have negative fantasies about the past or future, we can make ourselves very anxious. These memories and fantasies affect our beliefs and feelings, as well as our behaviour and what happens inside our bodies. In other words, they affect the other three parts of our script system.

If you keep thinking about negative memories (for example, an exam you failed) then you are likely to have negative thoughts (such as thinking you're stupid because you failed) and your outward behaviour and internal bodily experiences may be affected—you may start to get irritable or your digestive system may start to play up. Similarly, if you start fantasising that you are going to fail a future exam, the other parts of your script system could also be affected. There are three main differences between memories and fantasies:

⇨ memories are based on *real* situations, while fantasies are based on *imagined* situations

⇨ memories are only about the past, while fantasies can be about the past or the future

⇨ memories are realistic or possible (because you are remembering something that actually happened), while fantasies are often unrealistic or impossible.

Reinforcing memories

Let's consider your reinforcing memories first. Your adult insight will need to watch out and give you a big nudge when you start to dwell on your negative reinforcing memories around exam time. Firstly, you have to identify these memories, and then I will show you how to engage your adult insight to replace them with more positive ones.

Exercise 24: overpowering negative memories with more positive ones

In part A of this exercise you will be identifying your negative memories, then part B will encourage you to think of some positive memories. Finally, part C will encourage you to think of your negative memories in a different way. I have given our case study Sam's answers in italics as an example to help you.

Part A: identifying your negative memories

Look back at exercise 11 in chapter 3 and write down any memories you identified then. Add any more memories you can think of now. Remember that these memories can be related to any of the broad areas of exams, study, success, education and careers, as memories in any of these areas can lead to exam anxiety.

Sam might remember that his sister got through her exams without any difficulty.

You have probably been living with these negative and reinforcing memories for a long time and it will be hard to simply let them go or even to replace them with positive ones. Instead of spending energy trying to erase them, it will be more useful to add some new memories to your collection, so that you can shift your thinking to more positive experiences and not use all your energy remembering negative ones.

Part B: memories of positive events

Using your adult insight you can broaden your memory bank to include positive reinforcing memories. I want you to remember some happy times or events in the past that have nothing to do with exams or related areas. Think about times when you felt really happy and positive.

Sam might remember times when his swimming ability really shone through or perhaps when his parents made his birthdays special for him as a child.

Write down three or four of your own positive memories in your notebook.

It's also good to broaden your range of reinforcing memories to include positive ones to do with the areas of exams, study, success, education and careers. Try to think of positive memories, even though this may not be easy for you. You may not be able to remember a positive memory for each area, but see what you can come up with and write it in your notebook.

Sam might remember the time when his mother praised him for doing well in an assignment or when his school friend asked him for help with an assignment.

Write down positive memories about the following topics:

- ⇨ study
- ⇨ success
- ⇨ education
- ⇨ careers
- ⇨ exams.

Even though you may not have been able to think of a positive memory for each area, allow your mind to fill in the gaps over the next few days.

Part C: thinking of negative events in a different way

Some negative reinforcing memories (such as the ones you wrote down in part A of this exercise) may have been 'one-off' events, while others may have occurred fairly regularly. Looking back at part A, take each of the negative reinforcing events that occurred regularly and try to remember a time when you had a different reaction to them. Again, you may find it hard to remember a different response so allow your mind to fill the gaps over the next few days.

Sam might remember his sister often coming home saying that she got a good mark in her latest assignment. While he normally felt envious, there is one time he doesn't remember feeling any envy, rather he felt happy for his sister because he knew that she had struggled with the topic.

How to remember positive rather than negative memories

It's necessary to work at remembering positive memories, rather than trying to forget negative ones. As you remember positive events your mind will put the negatives into perspective, and even forget them.

Here are some things your adult insight can do to help you:

- write your positive memories on a piece of paper and regularly look at what you have written (keep a copy on your desk or as an electronic reminder on your computer's desktop)
- say the positive memories out loud to yourself, particularly when you catch yourself remembering the negative ones
- tell people you trust your positive memories.

Don't spend energy trying to erase negative memories, but rather use your energy to broaden your memory bank by adding new and positive ones.

Reinforcing fantasies

We will work on your negative reinforcing fantasies the same way we did with your negative memories. Firstly, we will identify your negative fantasies, and then broaden your range of fantasies to include positive ones. We will also make sure that your fantasies are realistic, otherwise you will just be perpetuating an unhealthy script system.

Exercise 25: overpowering negative fantasies with more positive ones

This exercise has two parts: identifying your negative fantasies and then replacing them with positive ones. Sam's answers are once again given in italics as an example.

Part A: identifying your negative fantasies

Firstly, look back at exercise 11 again, to remind yourself of the fantasies you wrote down. Next, in the left hand column of table 7.1, write down three negative fantasies you identified. Remember that your negative fantasies can be to do with areas including exams, study, success, education or careers, as negative fantasies in any of these areas can lead to exam anxiety.

Sam fantasised that his results were due to good luck rather than hard work.

In the middle column of the chart write 'past' if your fantasy was about the past or 'future' if it was about the future. In the last column write 'realistic' if your fantasy was realistic — in other words, it could very well have happened or it is possible for it to happen. Write 'unrealistic' if it was unrealistic (it could never happen). Be honest!

Table 7.1: your negative fantasies

Negative fantasy	Past or future?	Realistic or unrealistic?

Now that you've thought about your negative fantasies let's move on to broadening your collection of fantasies to include positive ones, remembering that these must be realistic and possible. Your new collection of fantasies should also be about the future, as we don't want to dwell on the past.

Part B: finding positive, future-oriented fantasies

As with memories, it is important not to spend energy trying to eliminate your negative fantasies, but rather to try to broaden your range of future-oriented fantasies that are realistic or possible. For this part of the exercise we will have to be creative about Sam's responses, as he was quite stuck in his negative fantasies.

What positive and future-oriented fantasies do you have that are *not* related to exams? If you can't think of any positive fantasies that you already indulge in, make a couple up now!

Sam might fantasise about the holiday he is planning to take over the summer or about going out with a girl he likes and who seems to like him.

It is also good to broaden your repertoire of reinforcing fantasies to include positive fantasies to do with the areas of exams, study, success, education and careers. Try to create some of these fantasies, remembering to keep them future-oriented.

Sam could fantasise about passing an exam he is anxious about or about the 'end-of-exam' party he and his friends are planning.

As with positive memories, if you can't create a positive fantasy for all areas, allow your mind to fill in the gaps over the next few days. Remind yourself that you are using your energy for more positive fantasies, rather than trying to get rid of negative ones. In this way you will move your balance towards the positive.

How to have positive, future-oriented fantasies

Here are some things you can do using adult insight to create positive, future-oriented fantasies:

- when you are not meant to be studying allow yourself the luxury of having one of the fantasies you described in exercise 25. You may not totally believe in it (even if it is realistic), but the more you can relax and fantasise about realistic future events, the more you will be making changes to the other areas of your script system

- describe a positive fantasy out loud, particularly when you catch yourself having negative ones
- tell people you trust about your positive fantasies.

Remember, don't spend energy trying to erase negative fantasies, rather use your energy to expand your fantasy bank to include positive and realistic ones about the future.

Hint: listen to track 3 on the CD

Track 3 on the CD is a positive fantasy that incorporates all four aspects of your script system. Now that you have learned to change your script it is time to listen to this track, as it will really help you move towards a positive script that will help you take your exams with no worries.

Positive visualisation

Track 3 brings together all aspects of your script system. By listening to this track regularly your beliefs and feelings will change, your internal bodily experiences will change, your behaviour will change and your fantasies about exams will change, all for the better. This track guides you through an imaginary journey of arriving outside the exam room, entering

Positive visualisation *(cont'd)*

it, doing the exam, and leaving the exam having completed it successfully. Sound unrealistic? Well, it's not. If you complete the exercises and follow the hints in this book this fantasy is very achievable.

Students taking an oral exam can also use this track but will need to personalise it. To do this, listen to it all the way through so you get the idea of the track. Then I suggest that you listen up to the point where you are asked to imagine yourself outside the exam room when you are centering yourself and preparing to go in. After this, turn the track off and imagine yourself doing your oral exam calmly and confidently as you engage with the people on your exam panel. Don't forget to see yourself at the end of your exam, heading off to reward yourself.

When you first start listening to the track you may feel anxious. If this is the case then you may need to listen to it several times. On the other hand, if you have conquered your exam anxiety by the end of part III then you may not feel any anxiety at all when you listen to it. You may even enjoy it!

The theory behind track 3 is that if you relax and repeatedly listen to a positive fantasy about some-thing that is making you anxious (in this case, an exam), you will finally be able to listen to it and not feel any anxiety. When you get to this point you will most likely not feel anxious in reality (in this case, when you sit the exam). For this reason, I want you to listen to the track as many times as it takes for you to listen to it without anxiety. You might feel a small amount of healthy psychological pressure (remember the graph in chapter 1?) but you must keep going until this is reduced to a normal and useful amount.

You will need about half an hour of uninterrupted time for this exercise, so when you have the time and space, settle yourself down and listen. Keep listening over the coming weeks until you can do so without feeling anxious.

Chapter summary

This chapter explained the difference between memories and fantasies. You also:

⇨ identified your negative memories

⇨ remembered more positive memories

⇨ remembered when you had a more positive reaction to a memory which was normally negative

⇨ identified your negative fantasies, including whether they were realistic or not

⇨ found more positive, future-oriented and realistic fantasies.

You were given hints on how to remind yourself of your positive memories and positive and realistic fantasies, and you also listened to track 3 on the CD to help you bring together all four aspects of your script system and make it work for you, rather than against you.

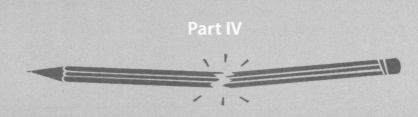

Part IV

How do I cope with the two big Ps?

Remember that fear always lurks behind perfectionism. Confronting your fears and allowing yourself the right to be human can, paradoxically, make you a far happier and more productive person.

— David M Burns

Do you procrastinate? — I'll think about it later!

— Anonymous

In the past when you've been through a stressful period in the lead-up to exams, you may have come across two major factors contributing to your problems: that you are a perfectionist, or that you procrastinate. If you have either (or both) of these tendencies, this part of the book is for you.

A perfectionist is someone who always wants to do a perfect job, while a procrastinator is someone who puts things off for no positive reason. These two big Ps can work individually or together to make your life a misery. As far as exams are

133

concerned, you may be anxious because you want to get a top mark, or because you have been putting off your revision. The more we put things off for no good reason, the more anxious we get.

If your goal is to get a top mark then you could well be putting off revision because the task you have set yourself is too hard and you are fearful that you won't be able to perform as well as you'd like. If you do manage to get a top mark then you could also pressure yourself to keep up this high standard, making your procrastination and perfectionist standards even worse.

Our patterns and our script system have a huge influence on our perfectionism and procrastination tendencies. Expectations to do well are often communicated to us directly ('Johnny, we expect you to get high marks') or indirectly ('Ryan got a high mark, isn't he great?'), usually when we are young, and we then go on to put pressure on ourselves to get high marks later in life. Some students may even rebel against these expectations and drop out of school, college or university.

Before we explore the issues of perfectionism and procrastination in more detail, let's look at a couple of examples of how students handicap themselves by being a perfectionist and procrastinator at the same time, and how this can make them anxious about exams. We'll start with Steven.

Steven

Steven comes from a family of doctors and lawyers. He managed to get a very high mark in his final school exams, which allowed him to train as a doctor. This was his goal, as well as that of his family.

Once at university, Steven felt high expectations from the medical faculty to do well. After all, it was an honour to be accepted into the course. He knew that he was privileged to have the necessary ability to become a doctor, but he also wished that he had taken a year off between school and university to give himself a break from study. He felt pressure from family and academics to get top marks, and he was also putting pressure on himself. He thought that if he was going to be a doctor he would have to be a perfect doctor at all times — people's lives would depend on him.

The amount of information Steven had to learn was huge and his assignment tasks were daunting. He often found himself staring at his computer, playing solitaire, or searching the net for unnecessary information. He felt unable to start his exam preparation because he didn't know quite where to start to get top marks. The more he put off his revision the more anxious he became.

Briony wasn't a 'top' student like Steven, but she still had issues with perfectionism and procrastination.

Briony

Briony secured her place at university through a special entry scheme that allowed final-year school students to enter on their report of the school rather than on marks gained through the exam system. She was overjoyed to secure a place in a business studies degree and hoped

Briony *(cont'd)*

to become an accountant. To do this, she would have to do well in the first year of her course so she could transfer to the accountancy stream of the degree.

When the end of school results came through, Briony had not done as well as she expected, but in her case the results were immaterial because she had already secured a place at university. However, she realised that she would have to put in more effort than she did at school if she wanted to transfer to accounting.

Briony worked hard because she wanted top marks — firstly, so she could transfer, and secondly to prove to other people that her school marks were a thing of the past and that she was capable of being a top university student. She set the stakes high — possibly too high — and put a lot of pressure on herself.

As well as studying, Briony also worked at a local supermarket to earn money to help finance her degree. Because she did this paid work so well (almost perfectly!) her employer offered her more shifts. This extra work was handy as it gave her more money, but it also meant that her revision timetable got away from her. She felt more pressure to revise, but she still accepted extra shifts. That way, she could blame any low marks she might get on 'having to work'.

Briony didn't have to work as many hours as she did. Her paid work became a vehicle for procrastination, while inside she was getting more and more anxious and dreaded her exams.

Both Steven and Briony were giving themselves a hard time and letting their perfectionist and procrastinating tendencies get in the way of allowing themselves to get on with the job of revision. They were both under pressure to do well, and in Briony's case her expectations may have been unrealistic.

The case of Ellie is very different.

Ellie

Ellie was not a top student at high school but passed well enough to get into university to study an arts degree. She has plans to become a librarian because she really enjoyed studying her Australian literature course and loves reading.

Ellie doesn't feel pressure to get top marks as she sees herself as a fairly average student, as do most people. She enjoys learning for learning's sake, and just wants to enjoy her courses. She does her best, gets on with her revision as exams approach, and also goes out partying with her friends when she needs a break. Because she doesn't pressure herself to get top marks and isn't self-critical, Ellie is comfortable allowing herself to not cover absolutely everything in her revision. As a result, she quite often surprises herself with higher grades than she expected. She has no big Ps getting in the way of her doing her personal best.

It is now time to look at these two harmful tendencies more closely.

Chapter 8

Coping with perfectionism

It is important to be clear about what it means to be a perfectionist. This chapter explores perfectionist tendencies, and the direct effect these can have on our level of anxiety.

Isn't it good to be a perfectionist?

Often people want to do a particular thing 'perfectly' for a reason—for example, they want to change a tyre perfectly so they don't cause an accident, or perhaps they want to perform a medical procedure perfectly so the patient is not in any danger. There is nothing wrong with trying to do something perfectly, particularly when lives are at stake; but when someone is *driven* by perfectionism, huge anxiety-related problems can occur.

The idea of being driven by perfectionism goes back to our patterns and script. We can take on board messages from significant people in our lives who urge us to strive for perfection. These people drive us to be perfect, particularly if we hear these messages (directly and indirectly) over a long period of time. Our borrowed messages become our own messages to ourselves, while our child responses make us anxious.

The idea of perfection is all around us in western culture. Apart from the significant people in our life, we also have the media publicising the perfect body, perfect beauty, perfect clothes, perfect cars and so on. It's suggested that perfection is what we should strive for, but the psychological (and financial) damage this message can cause is huge.

Of course, 'being perfect' (or at least 'being excellent') is highly respected in academic environments, so we have to battle these cultural borrowed patterns, too. Also, the higher we move up the educational system, the stiffer the competition and the harder the work. Perfectionists usually have a tougher and tougher time the higher they move up the academic ladder, as the goals they set for themselves seem to always be on the rise. If you do get a 'perfect' mark or wear the 'perfect' outfit then you have to keep doing it if you want to stay 'perfect'.

It is time for our adult insight to lend a hand. Our adult insight may help us strive for excellence in doing a task, or it may help us choose to do *our* best, rather than *the* best, but it won't allow us to drive ourselves into a huge stress attack if we are not perfect in all things. It is the persistent aspect of needing to be perfect that can be unhealthy and leave us with the belief that we are only good enough if we are perfect.

Perfectionists also find it hard to discriminate between tasks that have to be done as perfectly as possible and those that need not be done perfectly. For this reason, they can be seen to be not really in touch with the real world and its boundaries. On the other hand, people who strive for excellence on important tasks, rather than for perfection on all tasks, are more likely to have their feet firmly on the ground. For example, if you only have half an hour to do a job, you can choose to do that job as well as you can in that time period, or you can get really anxious because you won't be able to do a perfect job in half an hour. It's your choice, but let your adult insight help you out when you decide.

Perfectionism can lead to depression, social anxiety, exam anxiety, writer's block and many other afflictions. Jodi and Scott, the following case studies, both try to do their best with their studies, but Scott does so in a way that is much healthier psychologically.

Jodi

Jodi is a perfectionist. She has a little voice inside her head that's constantly telling her 'You must be the best', and sets unrealistically high goals that she always strives for and hardly ever reaches. She measures her self-worth entirely by what she has accomplished academically, and when she doesn't reach her goals she beats herself up about it and gets very anxious and depressed.

For Jodi, everything she does academically is equally important to her and she can't discriminate between tasks where she may have to accept a lower grade because of time or other restraints and tasks that she can devote more time to. To top it all off, on the rare

Jodi *(cont'd)*

occasions that Jodi does reach her goals, she uses her success as ammunition to strengthen her goals and this puts her under even more pressure. As you can imagine, exams are a nightmare for her.

Scott

Scott tries to do his best. He takes pride in his accomplishments and enjoys striving to do well — but he is not a perfectionist. He doesn't strive for unreachable goals, and doesn't measure his self-worth entirely by what he has accomplished academically. His self-esteem is formed by other things besides academic marks, such as his caring for others and his performance with friends in a band. The band isn't rated as the best, but Scott and his friends have a lot of fun practising and performing, and the bond between the members of the band is very supportive. Scott isn't hard on himself if he doesn't do as well as he hoped, and he is very pleased when he does reach his goals.

Remember that we are less likely to get anxious if we strive to do *our* best and forgive ourselves if we don't, but we will most likely get very anxious if we push ourselves to be *the* best at all times.

Exercise 26: estimating your perfectionist tendencies

This exercise will help you think about your own perfectionist tendencies. Table 8.1 contains 10 statements. Mark each statement according to how strongly you agree or disagree with it *most of the time*. Only choose one answer for each statement and respond according to how you usually think, feel and behave.

After you have marked each statement, add up your score for each column at the bottom. Finally, calculate your overall score, remembering that the plus and minus numbers cancel each other out.

Table 8.1: estimating your perfectionist tendencies

Statement	Agree strongly +2	Agree slightly +1	Disagree slightly −1	Disagree strongly −2
I am only 'good enough' if I get top marks.				
I am very scared of failing.				
I am hard on myself when I make a mistake.				
Perfection is painful but it's worth it — no pain, no gain.				
I can't draw the line under when to stop refining a piece of academic work.				

Table 8.1 *(cont'd)*: estimating your perfectionist tendencies

Statement	Agree strongly +2	Agree slightly +1	Disagree slightly −1	Disagree strongly −2
I can't draw the line under when to stop revising for an exam.				
Others achieve goals with far less effort than me.				
If one person thinks my work is no good, then everyone will think it's no good.				
I think grades are more important than learning.				
I find it hard to do just a 'good enough' job.				
Score for each column				
			TOTAL SCORE	

This exercise will only give you an indication as to the extent of your perfectionist tendencies. Ending up with a minus score would indicate that you do not have perfectionist tendencies, while ending up with a plus score would indicate that you do have these tendencies to some degree. Don't be hard on yourself if you have ended up with a plus score, as there is a bit of perfectionism in most of us. If you did get a high plus score, the exercises and hints that follow will help you lower it. The first step is to be aware of your perfectionism — now that you are aware you can do something about it.

Perfectionists tend to think in 'should's or 'must's. Look back at exercise 2 to see what you identified as your 'I should' and

'I must' statements. If you identified quite a few of these statements in the area of perfectionism then it's likely that your borrowed patterns have given you your perfectionist tendencies. It's important to weigh up the positives and negatives of being a perfectionist. You are asked to do this in the next exercise.

Exercise 27: identifying the advantages and disadvantages of being a perfectionist

Remember that you are trying to change the behaviour of being *driven* by perfectionism. As explained earlier, we all need to be as 'perfect' as possible with certain tasks, and our adult insight will prompt us to do this in certain situations. This does not mean we are driven by perfectionism. On the other hand, if our perfectionism is caused by borrowed and child patterns, our behaviour is definitely more driven. In these cases, we don't give ourselves a choice.

In your notebook, write down all the advantages of being a perfectionist. The answers from three earlier case studies have been provided as an example.

Steven might write that he wants to be a doctor, and doctors have to be perfect all the time; Briony might write that she wants to show others she is perfect after all; and Jodi might write that self-worth can only be assessed through academic results so her results have to be perfect.

Now write down the disadvantages of you trying to be perfect most of the time.

Steven might write that he becomes stressed when he can't remember; Briony might write that she takes on too much paid work in order to have a good excuse if she does not do well academically; and Jodi might write that she will never feel good about herself if she is a perfectionist.

There is a good chance that you identified far more disadvantages than advantages to being a perfectionist. Most people find being a perfectionist hard, stressful, time-consuming, lonely and, in the end, simply not worth it. As far as academic marks are concerned, most people do as well, or even better, when they are not struggling with the need to be perfect.

Sometimes, like Jodi, we only measure our self-worth through our academic achievements. We can't imagine finding satisfaction from anything else, unless we do this perfectly, too. It is important to realise and remember that we *can* experience satisfaction from things we don't do perfectly, and that this includes academic work, too. For example, Ellie enjoyed learning for learning's sake, and Scott enjoyed his experiences with the band.

Exercise 28: understanding your perfectionist tendencies and their effects

The point of this exercise is to help you understand that you can still experience satisfaction and self-worth from doing a task if you don't drive yourself to do it perfectly. When you don't put as much pressure on yourself you are far less likely to get anxious.

Part A of this exercise will ask you to think of three tasks you have done recently. The first task should be academic but the other two should not. Part B asks you what you have learned from doing this exercise.

Part A: identifying and answering questions on three tasks

Firstly, think of an academic task that you are currently working on or one that you did not too long ago and that you wanted to do really well. Examples could include doing an assignment or preparing for an exam. Write a brief description of this task in your notebook.

Next, think of a non-academic task that you have just done and which you also wanted to do well. Some possibilities are writing an important email or letter, cleaning something in the house or doing a job in the garden. Write a brief description of this task in your notebook.

Lastly, think of a non-academic task you are learning to do or have just learned to do. Some possibilities are learning to play an instrument or understanding your new computer software. Write a brief description of this task in your notebook.

Now write the answers to the following questions for each task in your notebook.

⇨ On a scale of 0 to 10, with 0 meaning doing the task most imperfectly and 10 meaning doing the task absolutely perfectly, at what score did you *want* to do each task?

⇨ Now using the same scale, at what score did you *actually* do each task?

⇨ How did each task affect your behaviour and mood? For example, did you feel frustrated or anxious, or have fun?

⇨ What would have happened if you had relaxed the standard you set yourself for this task?

Part B: identifying what you learned from this exercise

What did you learn from this exercise? Write your answers to each of the following questions in your notebook.

⇨ Were your scales and moods different for the academic task compared with the other two tasks? If so, why were they different? For example, do you think you drove yourself to do one type of task more perfectly? Did you put too much pressure on yourself? If so, what was the reason for this?

⇨ If you did put too much pressure on yourself in any of the tasks, was your resulting behaviour and mood worth it when you did so? Would your behaviour and mood be different if you relaxed your standards?

Making sure your goals are not driven by perfectionism

In chapter 5 I explained that in order to improve your concentration and lower your anxiety levels you need to make sure you set reachable goals and fulfil them regularly. These goals should be 'at least' goals — for example, 'I must do this at least before I take a break'. In order to keep your anxiety in check you must reach your goals most of the time, so it's very important that your goals are not 'perfect' ones all the time. Your goal setting must not be driven by your perfectionism, because wanting to do something perfectly usually creates a high degree of pressure. You may need to do a perfect job occasionally and for the right reasons, but don't let your goal setting be driven by perfectionism.

If you are still having trouble being realistic about your standards in the context of perfectionism, try exercise 29. This exercise will remind you how to challenge your belief systems. You have already done a similar exercise in chapter 6. In that exercise I asked you to identify some of your negative thoughts, to challenge them and to use your adult insight to find more useful thoughts to take their place. This exercise is similar but is only concerned with the idea of perfection.

Exercise 29: challenging your perfectionist tendencies

I will give you an example to remind you how to do this exercise before asking you to work out a couple for yourself.

Negative thought (about my perfectionism): I have to get top marks in the exam otherwise my parents will be disappointed, as I usually do very well.

Challenge: Why should you make yourself anxious just to keep them happy? What will happen if you don't get the top grade? What will they do? If they are disappointed will you be absolutely devastated?

Useful thoughts: It will be interesting to see how my parents react if I don't get the top grade—they may or may not be disappointed. If they are disappointed, at least I know that I have done my best and that I have looked after myself by not putting myself under too much pressure. I can always explain to them that I am doing my best to keep my anxiety under control at exam time. If their sense of self-worth is dependent on my success, that's their problem, not mine. And anyway, who knows what mark I'll get. I'll likely get the same mark even if I do set lower goals for myself.

Now try challenging your own perfectionist beliefs. Write your answers in your notebook.

It is also helpful to write out your useful thoughts and stick them somewhere you will see them regularly, or perhaps review your more positive statements before you sit down to revise. These thoughts can act as reminders when you feel yourself slipping back into your old perfectionist habits.

How to combat perfectionism

Below is a list of hints for combating perfectionism (most of these have been mentioned in the chapter, but if the idea is new there are a few words of explanation).

- Do a 'perfect' job only when it is really necessary.

- Set realistic goals, including 'at least' goals.

- Don't be afraid of failure if you lower your goals — most students do just as well even if they have lowered their goals.

- Watch your 'should's and 'must's. Do they come from adult insight or are they borrowed patterns?

- Take into account the circumstances you are studying under — remember that your best is not always the best.

- Don't try to cover everything when a deadline approaches. Instead, start with a 'broadbrush' approach and learn general principles, then (if you have time) go back and fill in the gaps. Give yourself permission to make mistakes — don't be harsh on yourself.

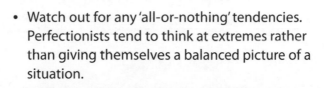

- Watch out for any 'all-or-nothing' tendencies. Perfectionists tend to think at extremes rather than giving themselves a balanced picture of a situation.

- Remember that just because one person thinks something is no good doesn't mean that everyone will think it is no good.

- Watch your moods and make sure that your study is not making you anxious or depressed. If it is, there's a good chance that your perfectionism is getting in your way.

- Remember to 'draw the line' at a reasonable time — perfectionists usually have trouble deciding when a job is complete.

- Have discussions with friends about the media's portrayal of perfectionism.

- Remember to put the emphasis on learning, rather than on marks.

Exercise 30: keeping your perfectionist tendencies in check

In your notebook write down anything that your adult insight has decided to take on board in order to keep your perfectionist tendencies in check.

In the following chapter we will deal with the other big 'P' word: procrastination.

Chapter summary

In this chapter you learned that:

⇨ perfectionism is a problem that plays a major role in exam anxiety

⇨ it's okay to want to do a task perfectly under some circumstances, but to want to be perfect all the time puts us under immense pressure

⇨ the need to be perfect all or most of the time is driven by our borrowed and child patterns and by our script.

In this chapter you were also given the chance to:

⇨ think about and rate your perfectionist tendencies

⇨ explore the advantages and disadvantages of being a perfectionist

⇨ understand that you can increase your self-esteem even when a job is done imperfectly

⇨ challenge your negative thinking about being perfect

⇨ learn how best to combat perfectionism.

Chapter 9

Stop procrastinating!

As with the perfectionist tendencies explored in the previous chapter, it is important to be clear about exactly what it means to procrastinate. This chapter explores procrastination tendencies, and the effect they can have on our feelings of anxiety.

What exactly is procrastination?

We procrastinate when we put something off for some reason to avoid doing it. Procrastination should be distinguished from purposefully delaying doing something for a *very good reason*. If we put off doing something because, for example, there is a higher priority we need to attend to (such as getting to the post office before it shuts to post something urgent), or perhaps because we are really tired and to try to do the task in this state would be a waste of time, then this is *not* procrastination, but rather purposeful delaying. In these two examples our adult insight has rationalised that it is better to put the task off for the time being.

As a rule of thumb, if our adult insight drives us to put a task off it is probably for a good reason, but if our borrowed or child patterns drive us to put the task off it is probably procrastination. Of course, we can rationalise via our borrowed and child patterns, too, so we need to be completely honest with ourselves when deciding whether or not we're procrastinating.

In this chapter, we will be returning to the borrowed and child patterns you identified earlier. Typically, borrowed patterns associated with procrastination come from significant people who were critical about us and perhaps told us that we were stupid, not good enough, or gave us other negative messages that we have taken on board. It might also be that significant people let us off the hook too easily and gave us permission to 'do it later'. From my work with procrastinating students I have found that they often use borrowed patterns from influential people in their lives, for example, 'I'm stupid', but sometimes they also use borrowed patterns that enable them to put things off, such as, 'it's a bit late to start now, I might as well leave it until tomorrow'. Caregivers who regularly give permission to delay tasks probably mean well, but may also cause procrastination problems later on in a student's life.

Our child patterns also cause us to procrastinate, particularly if they are working together with our borrowed patterns. For example, if a student feels scared of undertaking revision and ashamed that they can't just get on with it rather than putting it off, there are some powerful child patterns at work.

Because this book is about anxiety over exams, they will be our main focus; however, procrastination can be a mechanism we also use in other areas of study (such as doing an assignment) and can also spread to other areas of our life (such as cleaning the car). Mind you, the jobs that we normally procrastinate over, such as cleaning the car, often get done as a way of trying to avoid revision!

Exams have deadlines and, under normal circumstances, can't be put off. Some procrastinators rationalise their behaviour by telling others that they work best under pressure and that the exam has to be close before they can begin their revision. You now know that it is important to feel *some* pressure in order to perform well; however, it is usually necessary to start revision early in order for it to be effective and for you to actually remember what you are revising. In order to escape the trap of procrastination you need to use your adult insight to take control and change your habits, routines and mindsets.

Before going any further let's look at the case studies of two students who used to procrastinate.

Elise

Elise lives in a residential college attached to her university. College life is very social and she tends to easily get caught up in college activities, such as sports and watching TV in the communal lounge room. She has a close circle of friends who also live in the college. One friend in particular was going through a hard time in the lead-up to exams and Elise spent a lot of time supporting her.

Elise *(cont'd)*

On top of her social distractions, Elise was not confident in her academic ability and was unsure how to plan her revision. She also found some topics very boring. Instead of getting help with planning her revision she became very anxious, and distracted herself by spending too much time with her girlfriend and watching TV. She sent and received a huge number of text messages from friends who were living in other areas of the college or in town, and often slept in on the weekend. Through counselling, Elise learned to say 'no' to her friends, to only watch TV in her study breaks, and how to revise effectively. She went on to live at the college again the following academic year, but took with her the skills she had learned, including how to stay connected to her adult insight.

Alex has quite a different story, but he was also a procrastinator until he got help.

Alex

Alex, the eldest of three children, lives at home and attends a nearby university. His parents did not go to university and are proud of Alex for doing so and want him to do well. They tell family and friends that he is a 'very bright boy', but Alex knows that university is a struggle for him. His parents are also pleased that Alex is still living at home because they both work and need Alex to help around the house.

As his exams approached Alex became anxious. He did not think he would get the marks his parents were expecting and he felt overwhelmed by everything he had to revise. His parents encouraged him to study and said that they would take care of his jobs around the house until exams were over, but Alex kept doing his jobs, telling himself that his parents were very busy and needed his help—he was avoiding his revision. When his parents encouraged him to revise he replied that he would try, but when he did shut himself away to study he found himself playing computer games and surfing the net rather than getting on with his revision.

In desperation, Alex sought the help of a counsellor who helped him understand that he needed to set his own standards rather than judge himself by those of his parents. The counsellor suggested ways for Alex to revise, and helped him prioritise his revision above household tasks. He also encouraged the use of limited time on the computer as a reward after a revision session, rather than as a means of procrastination.

Notice that Alex said that he would 'try' to revise. When students use the words 'try', 'might', 'hope' or 'must' in the context of revision (or anything else for that matter), alarm bells ring in my head. It is patterns talking rather than adult insight. It is how a procrastinator talks. Procrastinators need to find out how to revise effectively and set goals to do so.

Some students revise and procrastinate at the same time by pretending to study, but avoiding the harder aspects of their revision—for example, they read but don't summarise, they look at revision exercises but don't do them, or they spend time photocopying and tidying their notes but don't actually read them. Some students avoid even useful forms of revision because they get anxious about getting anxious—for example, some students won't practise with past exam papers because they are worried they won't be able to do them and that this will make them anxious.

Let's get on with the job of finding out how much of a procrastinator you are, before moving on to the *how* and *why* of your procrastination, and the advantages and disadvantages of this behaviour. Once you understand your procrastination, we can look at ways to combat it.

The next exercise is similar to exercise 26, which helped you estimate your perfectionist tendencies.

Exercise 31: estimating your procrastination tendencies

This exercise helps you think about your tendency to procrastinate. Table 9.1 contains 10 statements. Mark each one according to how strongly you agree or disagree with it *most of the time*. Only choose one answer for each statement and respond according to how you usually think, feel or behave.

After you have marked each statement, add up your score for each column at the bottom. To finish, calculate your overall score, remembering that the plus and minus numbers cancel each other out.

Table 9.1: estimating your procrastination tendencies

Statement	Agree strongly +2	Agree slightly +1	Disagree slightly −1	Disagree strongly −2
I read more non-study-related magazines or books in the lead-up to exams.				
In the lead-up to exams I find myself doing jobs I normally put off.				
I play games, chat or send emails on the computer when I should be revising.				
I play games, text or talk on my mobile when I should be revising.				
I sleep more in the lead-up to exams.				
I avoid the harder aspects of my revision.				
I say 'yes' to requests when I should say 'no' so that I can revise.				
I overuse words like 'try', 'should', 'hope' and 'must'.				
In the lead-up to exams I make non-study activities last longer than they need to.				

Table 9.1 *(cont'd)*: estimating your procrastination tendencies

Statement	Agree strongly +2	Agree slightly +1	Disagree slightly −1	Disagree strongly −2
I feel anxious when I put off my revision.				
Score for each column				
			TOTAL SCORE	

The higher your score the more of a procrastinator you are. Ending up with a negative score would indicate that you do not have procrastination tendencies, while ending up with a positive score would indicate that you do. As with the perfectionist scale in exercise 26, don't be too hard on yourself if you ended up with a high score, as there is a bit of a procrastinator in all of us. If you did get a high positive score then the exercises and hints that follow will help you lower it. Once again, you will need to call on your adult insight to help you change your habits.

How do you procrastinate?

I have given you some typical examples of how people procrastinate in the previous case studies and exercise. To recap, typical ways of procrastinating include:

⇨ doing jobs that are a lower priority than your revision

⇨ taking more time to do things

⇨ avoiding the harder aspects of revision

⇨ watching too much TV

⇨ using your computer for non-study-related purposes

⇨ sending non-urgent emails

⇨ using your phone too much

⇨ going out with friends too often

⇨ sleeping too long.

Exercise 32: discovering how you procrastinate

In this exercise I want you to work out how you procrastinate. You may find that some of the ways you procrastinate do not correspond to those given in the previous list. Part A of this exercise will help you identify your five main time-wasting tasks, while part B will help you identify *how* you procrastinate. Your procrastination methods may or may not correspond to your time-wasting activities, but they will probably include them. Write your answers to the following questions in your notebook.

Part A: identifying your time-wasting tasks

In your notebook, write down your five main time-wasting activities.

Part B: identifying how you procrastinate

In your notebook, complete the following sentence.

I procrastinate by ...

Are there any similarities between your main time-wasters and how you procrastinate? If so, write them in your notebook.

Why do you procrastinate?

As we have seen, people procrastinate for all sorts of reasons, and these reasons can involve borrowed and child patterns. Here are some examples of why people may avoid revising for their exams:

⇨ lack of confidence in their ability

⇨ fear of being unable to meet expectations

⇨ not understanding the subject matter

⇨ not giving study top priority when necessary

⇨ being easily persuaded to take part in social activities

⇨ not enjoying the subject

⇨ thinking that they can't ask for help

⇨ because others tell them they *should* be revising.

This list is not exhaustive. The next exercise will help you identify your own reasons.

Exercise 33: identifying why you procrastinate

Below are seven questions for you to answer as honestly as you can. Once you have answered them you will be able to identify at least some of the reasons why you procrastinate. Write your answers in your notebook.

⇨ Look back at the five main time-wasting activities you identified in the previous exercise. What would you be doing if you weren't doing these activities?

⇨ How do you feel when you know you're wasting time?

⇨ What revision tasks are you avoiding when you do this?

⇨ Think about a specific study or revision task that you are avoiding. What specific aspects of the task do you find problematic (that is, difficult or unpleasant)?

⇨ Is there anything about the task that is not problematic, or perhaps even enjoyable?

⇨ Look back at your answers to exercise 2 and remind yourself of your 'should' and 'must' statements, particularly those you don't want to operate by (these were your borrowed statements). Do any of your answers shed light on why you procrastinate? If so, write down your insights.

⇨ Look back at your answers to exercise 7 and remind yourself of your child patterns around exams and how they affect you today. Do any of your answers shed light on why you procrastinate? If so, write down your insights.

After answering these questions you may be able to identify your reasons for procrastinating. Write down any reasons you have identified in your notebook.

The advantages and disadvantages of procrastinating

The biggest disadvantages of being a procrastinator (aside from simply not getting your revision done) are to do with feelings of guilt, shame and hopelessness. We can get stuck in our borrowed and child patterns if we're not careful, and the more we put off revision the more anxious we tend to get.

By now you will have identified exactly how and why you procrastinate. I have used the examples of Elise and Alex to help you understand the advantages and disadvantages of your behaviour below. Their responses are given in italics.

Exercise 34: identifying the advantages and disadvantages of procrastinating

In your notebook, write down all the advantages of being a procrastinator.

Elise might write that she feels good helping her friend, enjoys the time spent doing social activities, and doesn't have to face her lack of confidence. Alex might write that he feels good helping his parents, and doesn't have to face his fear of not being good enough.

Next, write down the disadvantages of procrastination.

Elise might write that she has feelings of anxiety and worries that she's lost control of her study. Alex might write that he is very anxious about exams, and procrastination worsens this anxiety.

Now that you understand how and why you procrastinate, it's time to move on to ways of combating this behaviour.

Combating procrastination

Sometimes overcoming procrastination is simply a matter of coaching ourselves through any natural resistance we have to doing something distasteful to us, and it is easier to do this once we understand the cause of our resistance. We confront our resistance all the time—for example, when we have to get out of bed on a cold morning, or when we have to eat breakfast quickly because we are running late. When we coach ourselves we do an activity that we find distasteful regularly; often we get into the habit of doing it. We can break the habit of procrastination over revision, too.

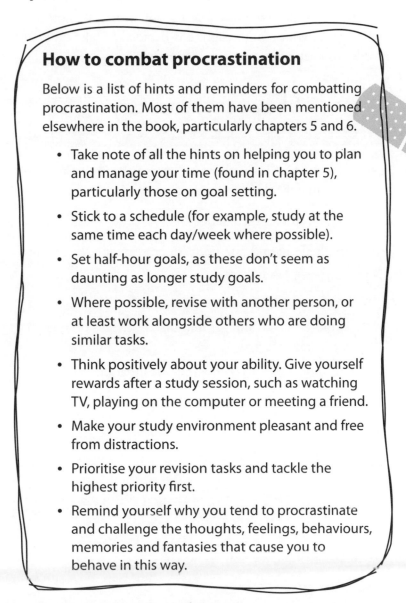

How to combat procrastination

Below is a list of hints and reminders for combatting procrastination. Most of them have been mentioned elsewhere in the book, particularly chapters 5 and 6.

- Take note of all the hints on helping you to plan and manage your time (found in chapter 5), particularly those on goal setting.

- Stick to a schedule (for example, study at the same time each day/week where possible).

- Set half-hour goals, as these don't seem as daunting as longer study goals.

- Where possible, revise with another person, or at least work alongside others who are doing similar tasks.

- Think positively about your ability. Give yourself rewards after a study session, such as watching TV, playing on the computer or meeting a friend.

- Make your study environment pleasant and free from distractions.

- Prioritise your revision tasks and tackle the highest priority first.

- Remind yourself why you tend to procrastinate and challenge the thoughts, feelings, behaviours, memories and fantasies that cause you to behave in this way.

Exercise 35: keeping your procrastination tendencies in check

To finish, I would like you to write down in your notebook anything that your adult insight has decided to take on board in order to keep you from procrastinating.

Chapter summary

In this chapter you learned that procrastination is a problem that plays a major role in exam anxiety.

In particular you had the chance to:

⇨ think about and rate your procrastination tendencies

⇨ work out how you procrastinate

⇨ work out why you procrastinate

⇨ explore the advantages and disadvantages of being a procrastinator

⇨ learn how best to combat procrastination.

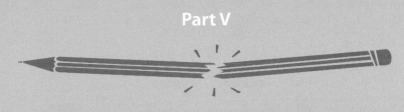

But I don't feel like a 'typical' student

Diversity is the one true thing we all have in common. Celebrate it every day.

—Anonymous

Due to political, economic and social differences, today's students are a diverse bunch. Part V addresses the issues related to exam anxiety that are faced by certain groups of students. For example:

⇨ many high school students go to school full-time and also work part-time. For this reason, they may experience similar issues to tertiary students

⇨ some students don't go on to university straight from school. Some have had a 50-year gap between the two

⇨ some students leave school at 16 and go on to tertiary study later through special entry schemes

⇨ university students no longer necessarily study full-time. Often they have time-consuming jobs and are trying to fit tertiary study around earning an income to enable them to study

⇨ sometimes students are enrolled in an off-campus mode and receive their qualification having never set foot in the institution in which they are enrolled

⇨ many students travel overseas to study in the senior high school and tertiary systems of their host country, only returning to their families when they have completed their study

⇨ many students come from overseas to learn English

⇨ some students moved to Australia after they began their education and have been educated in two or more cultural settings

⇨ the families of some students migrated to Australia years before they were born, but still hold on to their old culture, giving the student the benefits—and also the challenges—of living in two cultures.

The diversity of students today is reflected in our schools and other educational institutions. In addition, tertiary study is becoming more and more of a solitary occupation, as is illustrated by the growing number of part-time and off-campus students. Family, work and many other commitments can compete for time in a student's world and contribute to their anxiety over exams.

Part V contains five chapters and each chapter describes the issues faced by the particular group of students it refers to. Each chapter also gives special hints tailored for each type of student. Many students will need to read more than one chapter, as they are a combination of the various groups. Make sure you read every chapter that applies to you.

Chapter 10

Special hints for students mixing work or other commitments and study

To start with, let's look at four case studies of students who are juggling study and work or some other large commitment, and then explore the issues that can cause exam anxiety for them.

Sean is a full-time year 12 student who also works two part-time jobs.

Sean

Sean is tired and irritable. He has a paper round before school two days a week and he also works in the local pizza restaurant on three nights—and often has a weekend shift, too. His final year of school seems to

Sean *(cont'd)*

him to be full of exams and he is always rushing to get tasks done on time. His tiredness is affecting the quality of his revision, and he is arguing more and more with his family. He seems to be always walking around in a tired and anxious state, and as another set of exams looms his anxiety increases. Sean needs to learn some time management techniques in order to cope with his lifestyle, and this could well include letting one job go for the rest of the school year.

Matthew is an example of a student who is working full-time and studying part-time.

Matthew

Matthew is an exceptionally busy person. He works full-time for a computer company, but has realised that to get any further up the employment ladder he needs a degree. He is studying a computer science degree in his 'own' time, which means attending some lectures in the evening and studying most evenings and on weekends. He often says that he doesn't have a life. Depending on his timetable, he usually has to skip some lectures because he is meant to be at work. Matthew is enrolled as an on-campus student, but sometimes feels like he has enrolled in the off-campus mode. He doesn't really know any of the other students enrolled in his courses because he rushes in and out of classes and doesn't have time to socialise with anyone. Because of this, he doesn't know how his results compare to other students, or how other students are finding the course. Not knowing makes him anxious about his exams. Matthew is expecting to take about eight years to finish his degree.

Lucy has a fairly similar story to Matthew, although she doesn't have a full-time job.

Lucy

Lucy started studying for a diploma of fine arts at a local college at the beginning of last year. She decided to enrol part-time because her classes and assessment tasks take up a lot of her time, and also because the materials she needs for the course are expensive. As she is studying part-time, she is still enrolled in some first-year subjects. Lucy is putting herself through college, which means that she has to work a couple of casual jobs while studying. She works in the local fish and chip shop for about 15 hours a week and in a pub whenever she is needed. As both jobs are casual, she often doesn't know when she will be asked to work and sometimes misses classes to work a shift. She gets particularly anxious around exam time, especially if she is called in to work when she really needs to study

Another 'typical' part-time student is Mary. We will return to Mary again when we look at the issues facing mature-age students in chapter 12, but for now we will focus on her part-time enrolment.

Mary

Mary is studying to be a teacher. She is married with three children aged between six and 14 years. She and her husband decided that she would go to university once their youngest child had started school so she is now enrolled as a part-time student. It's going to be a long haul for Mary as it will take her about eight years to qualify as a teacher if she only studies part-time. She tries to attend classes and to study daily between the hours of 9 am and 3 pm when her children are at school—she jokes that she has regular school hours, too. Occasionally, Mary has to choose between not being home when her children get home from school and missing out on a class. When she does attend classes under these circumstances she often finds herself worrying about her children rather than concentrating on the task at hand. As exams approach Mary gets very anxious, and one reason for her anxiety is that she worries that her household will fall apart if she puts extra time into her revision. Her husband works long hours and so Mary is the one who cooks, helps with homework and cares for the children. Of course, this is why she decided to enrol part-time in the first place, but she still feels like it's 'crunch time' when exams draw close.

Time management is crucial

If you are enrolled as a part-time student you are probably trying to fit study around other commitments in your life. You may be working full- or part-time. You may have children, a family, or be taking care of other significant people in your life. Some students may not have any other time commitments, but have chosen to study part-time to keep the pressure off, as they know they don't handle it well. On the whole, part-time students are very busy people.

However you chose to mix study and work or other commitments, you need to understand that time management is crucial. If you manage your time well you will tend to be far less anxious about your exams and far more successful in them. If you are juggling your time you will know that you can't always study when you are at your most fresh, you often don't have large blocks of time in which to revise and you may also find availability an issue when you are trying to check things out with other students or your lecturers. Some students are shift workers and this adds another difficult dimension to the time management issue. Many part-time students tend to 'do it tough', but this chapter has extra hints and exercises to help you study and revise without getting anxious. You can be busy in other areas of your life and still study effectively.

For each of the following exercises you will need to know roughly how much time you are expected to spend on each subject per week. If you are an on-campus student you will need to know how much time you are required to spend in the classroom, lecture hall or lab—in other words, your contact hours. You will also need to know how much private study and revision time is expected of you to complete the required tasks. Your teachers, lecturers or course advisers will be able to give you some indication of how much time the average student needs for the course. This figure is usually around 10 hours per week in total for each subject that you are studying if you are at university, which includes class time and private study. Each course and institution is different, and of course each student is different. For example, if you know you are a slow reader you may want to add a couple of hours to your required study time to accommodate this.

It is important that you understand where study fits into your busy life. As you will know by now, to manage your exam anxiety you do need to attempt to balance your life as well as you can. You need to have leisure and pleasure and you need to focus on all your commitments equally. Achieving a balance in your life often requires planning; otherwise you can end up wasting valuable study and revision time by procrastinating.

Exercise 36: estimating how well you use your time

Let's have a look at what you are currently doing with your time. Take a look at table 10.1, which is a blank timetable. For this exercise you can either fill in the blank timetable provided, or you can make your own on paper or on your computer. The computer option has the added advantage of you being able to adapt the timetable to suit your own needs, and it is also possible to re-do the exercise as you start to make changes in how you use your time.

In the left hand column, you will need to fill in all your normal waking hours in hourly timeslots down the column (some students may prefer to make the timeslots half-hourly).

Special hints for students mixing work or other commitments and study

Table 10.1: my typical week at a glance

Time	Monday	Tuesday	Wednesday	Thursday	Friday	Saturday	Sunday

So, if you normally wake up at 7 am, make your first hour 7 to 8 am and finish at the time you normally go to bed. Notice that each of the other columns is headed with the day of the week. You should now have a blank timetable of your waking week.

Next, add all your regular commitments to the timetable—for example, put in all your class contact hours, paid employment hours, travel hours, the times you need to focus on your family, the times you play sport, and so on. In other words, create a snapshot of your typical week. If you are a shiftworker you may need to write out more than one timetable if your weeks tend to be different.

Now see if you have enough time left over in your week to study and revise. Do you have the required amount of hours available? If not, can you think of how you could rearrange your week to make time for study? Is there anything that can go? Is there anything you could pay someone else to do for you? Do you have any time for leisure and pleasure?

You may be wondering what all this has to do with exam anxiety—a lot. If we tell ourselves we don't have enough time to study then this can make us feel very anxious about exams. Going back to what you read about realistic and unrealistic threatening situations in chapter 1, it is important to make sure that, realistically, you do have enough time to study.

The next exercise will take the idea of realistic time management one step further.

Exercise 37: finding out if you use your time in your preferred way

In this exercise you will be working out some approximate percentages regarding how you use your time. Although you are only after an approximation, the following percentages may help. They are calculated based on eight hours' sleep.

At 16 waking hours a day for the seven days of the week:

⇨ 70 hours = 63 per cent

⇨ 35 hours = 31 per cent

⇨ 20 hours = 18 per cent

⇨ 10 hours = 9 per cent.

Think of your life as being divided into the following areas:

1   paid employment and associated travel time

2   academic study and associated travel time

3   home duties (this includes looking after yourself as well as others, and you need to take into account essential elements such as cooking, housework, gardening, shopping, and so on)

4   relationships with significant people (the time we spend doing things to enhance our relationships)

5   socialising

6   personal time.

Consider how you use your time each week *at the moment*. Put an approximate percentage of your time in the corresponding box for each area so that the total adds up to 100 per cent.

Actual time distribution:

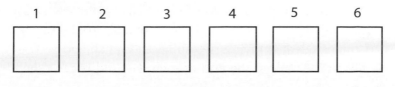

Sometimes we are not comfortable with the percentage of time we spend in one or more of these areas. In the next row of boxes, put percentages that reflect how you would *prefer* to spend your time. They may be the same as your actual distribution of time or they may not. Make sure any changes are realistic.

Preferred time distribution:

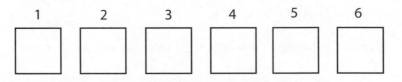

You have now had a think about how you *actually* spend your time and how you would *prefer* to spend it, taking into account the reality of your situation. If your two rows of boxes don't match up, what could you do to help your preferred distribution of time become reality? Write your ideas in your notebook.

If you are not happy with your distribution of time, are you prepared to make a contract with yourself to do your best to change it? If so, write the details in your notebook.

The final exercise on time management is about making sure you are spending enough time on each subject every week.

Exercise 38: estimating how much time you spend on each subject

Make yourself a chart like table 10.2. It would be best to make this table on a computer, as you will need a copy for each week of your semester. In the example given in table 10.2, Dave is a part-time student studying two subjects: French and geology. He fills in the table at the end of each day, and because he is an on-campus student he records how many hours he spent in class, and how many hours he spent studying outside of class (if you are an off-campus student you will only have private study time). Under each day of the week, 'C' stands for class contact, and 'P' is for private study.

Table 10.2: weekly timetable for Dave

Subject	Mon	Tue	Wed	Thur	Fri	Sat	Sun	Total
French	C/P	C/P	C/P	C/P	C/P	C/P	C/P	
	1/0	0/0	2/0	0/0	0/0	0/2	0/3	8
Geology	C/P	C/P	C/P	C/P	C/P	C/P	C/P	
	2/0	0/0	3/0	0/0	0/0	0/2	0/2	9
Total	3/0	0/0	5/0	0/0	0/0	0/4	0/5	17

Dave has four class contact hours for French and six for geology, but as you can see, he only attended three hours of French and five of geology in this particular week. As he is expected to do about 10 hours study for each subject, he really needed to do six hours of private study for French and four for geology during the week. Dave didn't quite make this target in the week of the example. Altogether he completed 17 hours of academic work, but he really needed to do 20.

As you go through the week, fill out your own table. If you keep up with your weekly tables this will make you aware of just how much time you spend on your academic work each week. If you are anxious and you know the number of hours you spend on academic work you can work out if you need to study more or if you need to challenge your thoughts and make them more realistic. Remember: exam-anxious students have usually studied enough to pass.

Patterns, script systems and the busy student

It is useful for students who find they are learning a lot in this chapter to have a good think about why they have chosen to juggle their life the way they do. Your choice may or may not have been influenced by your patterns and script system, but don't let yourself think that just because you made the decision to study this way you shouldn't challenge your reasons for doing so. I'm not suggesting that the reason for you making your decision is 'bad' or 'wrong', but that you must be clear about why you are having trouble juggling your time, and that you actually want to.

If it was your adult insight that guided you to this choice you will be a far happier student and, probably, a far more successful one. The following exercise will help you decide if it was actually your adult insight that guided you to your current time management practices.

Exercise 39: estimating how much adult insight you used when deciding to take on so much

To work out how much adult insight you used when deciding to take on so many roles, first answer the following question: why did you choose to take on so many roles? Write the answer in your notebook.

Now tick the most appropriate answer to the following question: how much adult insight did you use to guide yourself in making this decision?

☐ A lot

☐ A little

☐ None

☐ I don't know

Typically, the borrowed and child patterns of students struggling with conflicting commitments get in the way of their adult insight in the following areas:

⇨ perfectionism ('I must do everything in my busy life perfectly, including study')

⇨ procrastination ('work was really hard today so I'll revise tomorrow')

⇨ time management ('work should always come before study')

⇨ money ('I can't live on less money')

⇨ self-worth ('I shouldn't put my needs and wants before those of others').

Although most students these days want to gain qualifications for employment purposes, there are some people—particularly those who are retired—who simply want to learn for learning's sake. In general, these students are less likely to have time management, procrastination or financial issues around their study, but other issues may arise, such as needing to work their life as a student around other people in their household.

Revisiting the case studies at the beginning of this chapter, I described four very busy people. Some of the above issues may be getting in the way of their adult insight and they may need to change how they are going about their study. If this situation sounds familiar, do you need to call on your adult insight to make some changes?

Hint: how to juggle study and work or other large commitments

Below are some hints that you may find useful to help with the juggling act.

⇨ Ask for more flexible hours at work, particularly in the lead-up to exams.

⇨ Allow yourself to cut back on certain activities, making sure you are still able to maintain a balance in your life.

⇨ Learn to say 'no' to requests and invitations when you think the time would be better spent studying (your adult insight will help you decide when to say no).

⇨ Always allow some 'just in case' time when organising your time during crucial periods—'just in case a child gets sick' or 'just in case there's a crisis at work'.

⇨ Be prepared to live on less pay at critical study times.

⇨ Be willing to ask for help from others—be it academic, emotional or practical.

⇨ Talk to your 'significant others' (both at work and at home) in case they are not coping with your busy life. If they aren't, you will probably get anxious, so work out a solution to the problem.

⇨ Keep your long-term goals in mind. It is a long haul for most students who relate to this chapter, so when the going gets tough, remind yourself why you chose to study in the first place.

We will finish this chapter with one more exercise, as it's important to consolidate your ideas about why you are mixing study and work or other large commitments, and also to note any changes you are going to make to your thinking and behaviour around study to be a successful student.

Exercise 40: consolidating the ideas you gained from this chapter

In your notebook, complete the sentences below.

⇨ After reading this chapter I am going to change my behaviour by...

⇨ I am going to change the following thoughts about myself and my study...

⇨ My new thoughts are...

If your adult insight leads your thinking and behaviour around your busy life it will help you take your exams with no worries!

Chapter summary

In this chapter you:

⇨ learned that mixing study and work or other large commitments requires excellent time management

⇨ completed three exercises to help you manage your time effectively

⇨ considered why you have chosen to juggle your life in this way and explored your patterns and script system from this angle

⇨ were given some hints on how to mix study and work or other large commitments

⇨ made a promise to yourself about how you are going to change your behaviour and thoughts to help you cope with your busy life.

pathways
WWW.PATHWAYS TO EDUCATION.CA

Pinecrest-Queensway Health and Community Services
1365 Richmond Road, 2nd Floor
Ottawa, ON K2B 6R7
Ph: (613) 820-4922 Fax: (613) 288-3407

Chapter 11

Special hints for off-campus students

Students who are enrolled as off-campus students rarely—if ever—attend their educational institution. They receive their teaching materials and hand in assignments by post or electronically, their communication with teachers or lecturers is usually electronic or by phone, and they go to a designated venue to sit their exams. Off-campus students usually study part-time due to other commitments in their life. Sometimes they do so because they live in an isolated or remote area. As off-campus students can't schedule their time around contact hours, they need to be self-disciplined time managers.

Note: you must read the previous chapter before reading on.

Firstly, let's look at some typical case studies of off-campus students. We can then explore issues for off-campus students.

Maria and Michael

Maria and Michael live in rural New South Wales. They own a farm and both work hard on it. Their children attend boarding school because the farm is isolated.

Because of the drought and other weather problems, Maria and Michael decided they would like to sell the farm, as neither of their children seems keen on taking it over. Maria decided to gain a university qualification through the off-campus mode. She would like to work with animals so she decided to do an animal science degree. Michael noticed just how much she was enjoying her study and decided to join her not long after. He enrolled in a social science degree, with the view of possibly getting into local government employment.

So, Maria and Michael both work on the farm and are doing a couple of units a semester from a university that is located a long way away from where they live. Because of their isolation they can't talk to other students easily and for this reason they often feel cut off from the university, even though there are people employed there for them to contact if necessary.

Both are anxious about their exams and feed off each other's anxiety. Maria is the type of person to show her anxiety, whereas Michael tends to hold his in. As exams approach he seems to get angry easily and this puts even more stress on their situation.

Another type of off-campus student is Seria.

Seria

Seria is a physically disabled student. She is a paraplegic and is confined to a wheelchair. After she finished high school, Seria decided it would be best if she enrolled in the off-campus mode to do a full-time degree in arts, as physical access was a problem for her. Seria lives near her university and occasionally visits the campus, but usually studies at home with her off-campus study materials. Even so, she sometimes feels very isolated, particularly as exams approach, so she does her best to talk to other students and her lecturers to overcome this. Seria doesn't have any other large time commitments and lives at home with her family, who are very supportive.

Some off-campus students simply want to learn for learning's sake. They have retired from employment and can finally study subjects that interest them. Robert is one of these students.

Robert

Robert is in his 60s and has always wanted to learn French. He never thought he had the time to do this while he was working, but has now decided that he will make it a retirement project and study in the off-campus mode, as there is no university offering the subject nearby. He talked to his wife about the idea and she was initially very supportive.

Robert *(cont'd)*

As time went on, Robert began to spend more and more time shutting himself away to study. He attended 'on-campus days' and joined a local French-speaking group to improve his conversational French.

After a while Robert's wife felt left out and angry and became quite jealous of his new 'hobby', and she began to place demands on him to do more around the house. As Robert's exams approached, his wife became even more difficult, and Robert felt torn between studying and spending time with her. He is now anxious about his exams, as he thinks he is not doing enough revision.

These case studies are fairly typical of off-campus students and the problems that are associated with this mode of study. Of course, many students are different. They may work full-time and decide to do their degree slowly by off-campus mode because they can't get to lectures, even though their university is close by. Many others are parents with children so they can't easily attend classes, and others are shiftworkers who find it impossible to fit their classes around work. What they all have in common is that they are studying in isolation.

Don't drop out!

As you can imagine, the drop-out rate for off-campus students is highest in their first semester. Apart from learning their subjects, they also have to learn how to fit study into their lives and around their loved ones. Many students didn't realise the impact that off-campus study would have on their lives; however, if they can survive their first semester the path normally gets easier from there. Exams bring extra stresses and strains for off-campus students, and this is what we will be looking at in this chapter.

Time management for off-campus students

Almost all that I have written about time management in chapter 10 also applies to off-campus students, so make sure that you have read it and done the exercises before reading this chapter.

As you are an off-campus student and don't have classes to attend (unless you attend any on-campus days) it is very easy for time to get away from you. Even though your lecturer will give you a timetable of academic work to follow, it is up to you to stick to this schedule. Many students find this hard to do, and before they know it exams are upon them and they are anxious about not having done enough work. For this reason, it is also important that you have read chapter 5, as it gives you lots of ideas on how to manage your study time.

In chapter 5 there was also information on goal setting, which is particularly important for off-campus students. In the off-campus mode there are no classes to prepare for and attend, so you have to be very disciplined and follow realistic goals you have set for yourself. Weekly goals are particularly important. Often off-campus students choose this mode of study as their weeks are never the same because of shift work or other issues. If this applies to you, choose a time (for example, Sunday evening) to make a decision about when you are going to study during that week—and stick to it! Also, if you are doing more than one subject, make sure that you study *each* subject each week. Sticking to a regular weekly goal system will help you manage your anxiety around exam time.

As an off-campus student, it may be tempting to just work on the end of the kitchen table or similar—don't! Make sure you set up a space that is yours alone and make sure that no-one disrupts it. This is a place that you can retreat to when you get the odd five minutes to revise using a five-minute goal.

Studying in isolation

Off-campus students usually feel isolated regardless of where they live in relation to their educational institution. They often say that even though there are people all around they still feel alone. They may even be in regular contact with their lecturer, but still feel isolated.

If this is the case for you, it is extremely important that you feel comfortable enough to ask for help. If necessary, re-read the section on asking for help in chapter 5, which included tips on asking for academic and emotional support, finding out about exams and setting up a study group. Off-campus students often find it helpful to set up study groups, although they may have to be by telephone or via the internet. Off-campus courses usually offer ways for students to contact each other and their lecturers by email, so take advantage of this, too.

Remember that anxiety is fuelled by the unknown, so try to make the unknown as known to you as possible. Some off-campus students also find it helpful to talk to other students, past or present, even though they might not be studying, or have not studied, the same subjects. Off-campus students can certainly help each other deal with common issues. You don't have to feel alone.

Communicating with those close to you

Remember Robert from the previous case study, who was studying French? Robert's wife supported him initially, but soon she resented the time he took out of their life together in order to study. This is a common problem and it is not just partners and spouses that can feel resentful, jealous or hurt. Children, close friends, workmates and even work supervisors can also feel this way. Realistically, there are going to be times when you have to shut yourself away to study or revise, and these times will probably increase as exams get closer. For some students there will also be on-campus days to attend. It is important that you discuss the demands of your course with those close to you before you enrol — and to keep talking to them as the course progresses. It is usually only when those close to you feel okay about you studying that you will be able to focus on your revision and manage your anxiety over exams.

Patterns, script systems and the off-campus student

The patterns and script systems that cause exam anxiety in off-campus students are exactly the same as those found in exam-anxious students who study on campus. Because of the additional issues that off-campus students have to deal with, anxiety over exams is a common problem with this type of student. As most off-campus students are also part-time, the typical borrowed and child patterns are the same as those outlined in the previous chapter. Perfectionist tendencies, procrastination, time management, money and self-worth issues all contribute to feelings of anxiety.

Working in isolation is difficult and can act as a catalyst for pattern and script system issues. For example, it can be hard to negotiate study time when you don't have a class to attend. Students with low self-worth ('the needs of others should come before my own' or 'if I take time out for study my partner will get upset') may find it hard to take the time they need for study, which can lead to feelings of anxiety about their exams.

In addition, asking for help is difficult for many students, as is asking others how they are coping with your study commitments. Imagine a student with a borrowed pattern of 'only weak people ask for help' and a child pattern of 'I'm scared I'll be laughed at if I ask for support'. They would find the off-campus mode particularly difficult.

One issue common to off-campus students is having issues identifying themselves as students. They don't have a sense of belonging as a student because they never see other students or attend campus. This is a very real problem and another reason why it is important to join any electronic list or chat room created for students in your course.

Interestingly, some students choose to study in the off-campus mode because they are loners; they prefer to remain alone and feel very uncomfortable talking to others. The off-campus mode suits them perfectly. By now you may be able to guess the sorts of patterns that these students operate from, but keep in mind that we can only guess and we won't know for sure unless we talk to them in depth. They may have chronic anxiety, with exam anxiety being just one of the many issues they face.

If any of the issues described in this chapter are getting in the way of your successful study in the off-campus mode, I suggest you look carefully at what is driving these difficulties. The next exercise will help you to use your adult insight to understand what is getting in the way of your studying.

Exercise 41: understanding how your patterns and script hinder your study in the off-campus mode

In chapter 3 you discovered the content of your borrowed and child patterns and your script system. This exercise asks you to relate this knowledge to your way of dealing with studying in the off-campus mode, particularly (but not exclusively) in the area of exams. If necessary, look back to the exercises you did in chapter 3 before you complete the sentences below in your notebook.

⇨ My borrowed patterns interfere with my studying in the off-campus mode and therefore my exams by ...

⇨ My child patterns interfere with my studying in the off-campus mode and therefore my exams by ...

⇨ My script system interferes with my studying in the off-campus mode and therefore my exams by ...

You will be given the chance to make a contract with yourself to change these habits after reading the following hints.

Extra hints for off-campus students

All the hints given in chapter 10 are also relevant to off-campus students and I have expanded on many of them in this chapter. Here are the additional hints for off-campus students in particular.

⇨ Make sure you set a regular time of the week to decide when you are going to find time to study in the next week—and stick to your decision.

⇨ Make sure you study all your subjects each week. Don't fall behind in any of them.

⇨ Find a place of your own to study, however small it may be.

⇨ Make sure you fully understand how the off-campus mode will, or does, impact all areas of your life.

⇨ Ask for emotional and practical support when you need it.

⇨ Make sure that people close to you are coping with your study commitments.

We will finish this chapter by doing one more exercise. It is important to consolidate any ideas that you have formed while reading this chapter, and to make note of any changes you want to make to your thinking and behaviour with relation to study.

Exercise 42: consolidating your new ideas about off-campus study

In your notebook, finish the following sentences.

⇨ I have chosen to enrol as an off-campus student because...

⇨ After reading this chapter I am going to change my behaviour by...

⇨ The thoughts I am going to change about myself and my study are...

⇨ My new thoughts are...

If your adult insight leads your thinking and behaviour with regards to the way you tackle your study as an off-campus student, it will help you take your exams without anxiety.

Chapter summary

In this chapter you learned that off-campus students:

⇨ must be self-disciplined time managers

⇨ should have a place of their own to study

⇨ must learn how to fit study into their life and around their loved ones

⇨ must regularly communicate with the significant people in their lives to make sure these people are coping with their study

⇨ can feel very isolated even if they live close to their educational institution

⇨ must ask for help when needed.

In addition you:

⇨ learned how your own patterns and script system can hinder your study in the off-campus mode

⇨ were given extra hints on how to cope with this mode of study

⇨ consolidated your ideas about coping with off-campus study so that your exam anxiety is lessened.

Chapter 12

Special hints for
mature-age students

Mature-age students are normally defined as those who start their tertiary study aged 21 or over. Some may be a lot older, having decided to do some tertiary study for the first time only once they have retired—like Robert in the previous chapter. Many mature-age students are juggling several commitments, may be studying in the off-campus mode, may have recently migrated or may be international students. Remember to read every chapter in part V that applies to your situation.

Options of entry for mature-age students

There are several different ways to gain a place at university, though not all of the following are offered by all institutions.

Some students dive right in, applying through a mature-age entry scheme, where all they have to do is fill in an application form. Some schemes require a little more effort than this, such as writing an essay, having an interview or completing an aptitude test. Some students opt for a condensed course of schoolwork that is offered by some colleges. Others enrol in a tertiary preparation course, which helps them with subject matter, study skills and orientation to tertiary study. And of course some have already completed some academic study at tertiary level.

Many tertiary institutions have an 'open door' policy that allows prospective mature-age students to dive straight in to study. Unfortunately, this 'open door' becomes a 'revolving door' for many students because they leave before completing their studies. Students drop out for any number of reasons, one of them being anxiety over study — particularly exam anxiety. Most students feel some sort of self-doubt before starting college or university, but for many mature-age students this self-doubt is enormous. This chapter will help you overcome these issues in order to study successfully.

The statistics being released by counselling services in tertiary institutions show that mature-age students are over-represented as clients for these services, which is a good thing. Mature-age students seem to realise that they do need help and are willing to go to a counselling service to get it. Make sure you do, too, if you think things are not going as smoothly as they could be.

Let's look at some typical mature-age students, starting with Mary, who we met in chapter 10. Re-read her case description on page 172.

Mary

What I didn't tell you earlier is that Mary left school at 16, married early and has devoted her entire life to looking after her husband and their children. She saw her enrolment at university as a chance to prove to herself and to her family that she has what it takes to become a teacher. She also decided (together with her husband) that she needed to work to help pay off their mortgage and save for their children's education. As you can see, the stakes were high for Mary.

When Mary first came to the university's counselling service it was because she was anxious about her upcoming exams. She told the counsellor that she couldn't think straight or remember anything she revised. You learnt in chapter 10 that Mary was worried her household would fall apart if she devoted extra time to her revision, but she was also worried about what her family would think if she failed the course — and about the financial implications of failing. As a result, she was having trouble sleeping and was very irritable towards her husband and children.

Mary's case is a fairly typical example of some of the stresses that mature-age students can face when they decide to return to study. Let's examine a couple more case studies before looking more deeply into the typical pressures these students can experience.

Glen

Glen was 44 when he was made redundant, along with most of the people he worked with. He had been a supervisor at a car manufacturing plant, and helped many of his coworkers get through the trauma of their own redundancy. Glen did a great job in helping this way, so after talking it over with his wife, he decided to use his redundancy payout to retrain in personnel services. He enrolled in a degree in human resources and entered university as a mature-age student. Glen had left school early and was admitted to university under a special mature-age student scheme, which simply required him to write an essay explaining why he wanted to do the course.

Glen found academic work hard and often wondered if he was on the right track. He saw himself as older than the other students and struggled with the fact that even the lecturers seemed younger than him. He never spoke up in tutorials and seminars because he didn't want to appear stupid. He came to the counselling service because he was getting more and more anxious about his academic ability and was particularly worried about his exams—he hadn't taken one since he was about 15 years old.

Our next case study, Diane, entered university in a different way to Glen, but is still a mature-age student facing her own unique pressures.

Diane

Diane is a single mother of one young child. She wants to fulfil her dream of going to university; a journey she put off when she found out she was pregnant. She is now in her 20s so when she felt her child was old enough to go into day care she enrolled in a tertiary orientation qualification at a local college, which was her pathway into university.

Diane chose to enter university this way because she thought the transition from this course to university would be easier than applying directly. In many ways it was, but once she was well into her first semester at university she realised that she was not getting the direction she needed from the academic staff and that the course was going too fast for her to keep up. It was certainly not like the course she had done at college in this respect.

Even though she thought she was floundering, Diane talked a lot in tutorials and seminars because she hated the silences that occurred when the younger students wouldn't speak up. Sometimes she thought that the younger students were angry with her for doing this — even though they told her they were pleased she was doing all the work! It was the speed of the course that worried her most, and she was very concerned that she would not catch up in time for her exams. Her anxiety about exams increased so much that she consulted the university's counselling service.

Special issues for mature-age students

Mature-age students face special issues, as illustrated in the previous case studies. Mature-age students:

⇨ may have left school many years ago

⇨ may not have finished high school

⇨ may enter tertiary education through a pathway that has prepared them in some way

⇨ usually have given up some financial security to embark on the relatively unknown

⇨ usually have to juggle several roles in a busy life

⇨ may have moved closer to the institution, with or without their families or partner

⇨ usually have higher stakes to succeed

⇨ often have a fear of failure

⇨ probably have real—or perceived—pressures to do well

⇨ usually need a lot of support from friends, family and professionals, especially at the beginning of a course

⇨ probably worry about their age compared with other students and academic staff

⇨ probably worry about how much they speak up in seminars and tutorials

⇨ have not taken the decision to enrol lightly

⇨ are usually pleasantly surprised at how many other mature-age students there are

⇨ are often highly anxious around 'crunch times'.

Some research on mature-age students

The good news is that research shows that although mature-age students are often more anxious and concerned about failing than students who start university straight from high school, they usually do much better than these students because they are more experienced, mature and motivated. If mature-age students can get through their first semester and all the adjustment problems that arise in this period, they usually do very well.

The academic and administrative staff who work at educational institutions understand what the educational culture and experience is all about, but mature-age students usually do not. For this reason, many mature-age students find the whole experience quite daunting at first. Research shows that if mature-age students feel validated and supported by their family, teachers and lecturers they are more likely to do well, so support is vital. Some mature-age students see their attendance at a tertiary institution as a 'second chance' or 'an opportunity not to be missed'. In addition, if the student is first in their family to go to university then they tend to work particularly hard to prove themselves. As you will now realise, feeling daunted, needing validation and support, and working very hard to do well are all ingredients for a big dose of exam anxiety for mature-age students.

From the above list of possible pressures you can see that many of them are sociological in nature. Many of these pressures are also very real—for example, juggling roles, financial issues, moving house, not having studied for a long time, and so on. In addition, many older mature-age students tend to worry about their memory. While it's true that memory does decrease with age, it's also true that if we use strategies to improve our memory then the effects of age can be lessened considerably. Chapter 5 is full of strategies to improve your memory, including active learning, lots of recall and short study sessions.

Patterns, scripts and the mature-age student

In my experience, the psychological pressures of patterns and script systems on mature-age students are often very challenging and can lead to a huge dose of anxiety, particularly at exam time, simply because the stakes are so high. I have found that mature-age students, as a group, tend to be more perfectionist than students who come straight from school, so it would be worth re-reading chapter 8 on perfectionism if this applies to you.

When we find ourselves in a difficult situation our borrowed and child patterns often rear their heads and our script system springs into action.

Borrowed patterns

Typical borrowed patterns of mature-age students include:

⇨ I must be able to prove to others that I can succeed

⇨ I should do as well as my brother (or sister)

⇨ I must get top marks

⇨ I must raise my kids perfectly, even though I am studying

⇨ I should not let my study interfere with the running of my household

⇨ I should do better than students who are the same age as my children

⇨ I must keep up with all my other commitments.

Remember that borrowed patterns are full of 'shoulds' and 'musts' and can make students feel very anxious. It is important that you challenge your beliefs and decide whether you want to live by them. Rather than giving you another exercise to do, look back to exercises 1 and 2 in chapter 3 to make sure you are no longer operating from borrowed patterns, but from your adult insight.

Exercise 43: identifying which borrowed patterns your adult insight needs to watch out for

In your notebook write down any thoughts, feelings or behaviour that your adult insight needs to watch out for because they come from your borrowed patterns. Remember that borrowed patterns tend to re-emerge when the going gets tough until they are knocked on the head once and for all.

Child patterns

Child patterns can re-emerge when we are feeling stressed because we are in an unfamiliar environment, and this is often the case for mature-age students in the rather daunting environment of their first semester at university. Some typical child patterns include:

⇨ If I don't do well my family will say 'I told you so'

⇨ I'm scared to ask for help and support because it will make me look stupid

⇨ I'm scared to talk to my partner about my study because they may say they are not coping with it and then I'll feel terrible

⇨ I should keep my anxiety to myself

⇨ I will be anxious about my exams

⇨ everyone is watching to see how I'll manage

⇨ I was never 'good enough' for my parents, so now I won't be 'good enough' to pass.

The above list illustrates a couple of issues that are worth highlighting. As mature-age students do much better if they feel supported and validated by their family, friends and the staff at the institution, it is important for them to ask for support if it is not forthcoming. Many mature-age students get into the mindset that they 'should' be able to do well without asking for help, and that asking for help somehow makes them appear weak. These are powerful borrowed and child patterns at work. It is important to be able to ask for help when you need it, or to see a counsellor if you have trouble doing so.

The other issue worth highlighting is also related to communication. It is vital that you keep talking to your family and other significant people in your life to make sure they are coping with your study commitments. I have seen many clients who confided that their partner or family said that they would support them in their studies, but that, as the semester or year progressed, the support disappeared. It is essential that you keep talking to those close to you so that if they are no longer coping you can work out strategies to help them. Sometimes child patterns set in and communication stops or doesn't happen easily. Watch out for this issue and ask for help if you need it.

Exercise 44: identifying which child patterns your adult insight needs to watch out for

Exercises 3 to 7 in chapter 3 helped you get in touch with your child patterns and so, as with borrowed patterns, I won't repeat them here. Instead, write down any thoughts, feelings or behaviour your adult insight needs to watch out for because they stem from your child patterns in your notebook.

Script system issues

You explored your script system in chapter 2, so take another look at that chapter to see what you discovered back then. Remember: mature-age students have more memories than those coming straight from school! In my experience, mature-age students are also more easily able to identify internal warning signs of anxiety. Some say that mature-age students are more set in their ways than younger students, and if this is the case, you will recognise your outward behaviour much more easily. Your beliefs and feelings about yourself, others and the world have all been explored with the patterns you identified earlier.

Exercise 45: identifying the script system issues your adult insight needs to watch out for

Use your knowledge of your script system to make a note in your notebook of what your adult insight needs to watch out for so that these issues don't become a major problem.

Extra hints for mature-age students

Read all the hints I mentioned in the previous two chapters, as they are all relevant to you. In addition:

⇨ remember that there are other mature-age students. Find them and share your experiences with them

⇨ remember that the first semester is particularly important. Not only do you have to study, you also have to learn how to juggle study and your life outside of being a student

⇨ watch out for any perfectionist tendencies

⇨ use the strategies to keep your memory in good order—use it or lose it

⇨ ask for support if you are not getting it

⇨ make sure that people close to you are coping with your study commitments

⇨ use the counselling service at your institution for support and guidance, if necessary.

A final word for mature-age students

You may be wondering about the issue of speaking up in class. Some mature-age students, such as Glen (a case study at the beginning of this chapter), stay very quiet in class. Others, such as Diane, speak up a lot, either because they have a lot to say or because they hate silences. There is no 'rule' about this. On the whole, mature-age students tend to speak up more than those coming straight from school. Check this out with the other students in your class once in a while, and ask for their opinion. Most school leavers are relieved that the older students speak up as it means they don't have to! Of course, academic staff should guide the group so they all contribute equally, but this does not always happen. Some academic staff are quite a lot younger than their mature-age students, and may even feel intimidated by them!

Chapter summary

In this chapter you learned that mature-age students:

⇨ may have arrived at a tertiary institution via one of several pathways

⇨ usually have more self-doubt, fear of failure and anxiety than students who come straight from school, but usually perform better than school leavers

⇨ worry about their memory, but by using certain strategies the effects of age on their memory can be lessened considerably

⇨ need to communicate with the significant people in their lives to make sure these people are coping with their study commitments

⇨ have often not taken the decision to enrol lightly, which raises the stakes to do well

⇨ need help and support, especially at the beginning of their course

⇨ are fairly numerous on campus

⇨ are over-represented as clients in campus counselling services, which is a good thing.

In addition, you:

⇨ asked your adult insight to watch out for old patterns and script system issues

⇨ were given extra hints to cope with being a mature-age student.

Chapter 13

Special hints for international students

This chapter is for students who have come to Australia on a student visa to study at an educational institution, be it at high school or tertiary level. Some students come to learn English before transferring to university or college, while others go home after finishing their English language course. Some courses are private and others are paid for by the government. All international students have one thing in common: they have voluntarily come to their host country for a set period of time as a student, and are expected to return to their home country at the end of their course.

International students have issues specific to their situation that can cause exam anxiety, in addition to the general issues explored in this book. The pressures to pass are very real and the pressure to succeed is usually extremely high. Before discussing the special issues, let's look at some case studies of typical international students.

Rashid

Rashid is from Malaysia and is 23 years old. He is a private international student studying for a bachelor's degree at university. He is in his second year of study, but is repeating two subjects that he failed in his first year. His English is good, but initially he had problems adjusting to the Australian culture and its educational system, which is probably why he failed the two subjects. He finds it hard to think for himself, and prefers to copy his lecturer's opinions instead. His parents — correctly — believe he is very intelligent and are investing a lot of money in paying his expensive education fees. His family, friends and colleagues back home are envious of his opportunity to study overseas. Rashid consulted a doctor because of stomach problems and the doctor referred him to the university's counselling service, as he believed Rashid's problems were caused by extreme stress. His exams were very near and Rashid asked the counsellor and doctor to support an application for his exams to be put off until the next semester, as he was ill and needed more time to study.

It is a well-documented fact that international students from non-western countries tend to avoid counselling services, preferring to see a doctor instead. The 'internal bodily experiences' part of their script system is a very good indicator of the anxiety they are experiencing.

Mee

Mee is from mainland China and is in her first year of university in Australia. She had been here for seven months when she first used the counselling service. She was homesick, having left all her family and friends in China, and was not expecting to return home until she completed her degree. English is not her first language and she is slow at reading and writing it. She is also scared of speaking up in class because she thinks she won't be understood.

Mee is not used to western-style food, but lives with other Chinese students, so they can cook Chinese cuisine for themselves. Her first semester exam results upset her because she failed one subject and only just passed the other three. The other Chinese students seem to get much better marks. When the counsellor met her Mee was feeling ashamed, humiliated and had difficulty admitting failure. She was finding it hard to face the other students and had not told her parents about her results. The thought of her next exams was making her feel very anxious.

As in Mee's case, international students can face very real difficulties with the English language. In addition, the feeling of shame, or 'losing face', is very common for students from some cultures.

The next case study is an example of yet another type of international student.

Renato

Renato is from Brazil and is in Australia to learn English at a private institution attached to a university. The arrangement is that if Renato passes his English language exams he will be allowed to go to university to do a masters degree. He spoke very little English before he arrived, and was living with an Australian homestay family who speak no Portuguese, so it was initially very difficult to communicate with them. He was in a stressful situation so his anxiety over exams was heightened.

Renato needs to pass his exams to enrol in his masters course and sometimes he thinks this will never happen. He is so stressed that he can't see the progress he is making with learning English. Whenever he has to sit a test (which is frequently), he gets very nervous and can't remember his vocabulary and grammar.

Whatever type of international student you are, you will know that adapting to a new culture and language is usually a very difficult and stressful thing to do. Add exams to the mix and anxiety is usually the result. This chapter is designed to help you overcome this and to succeed as an international student.

Dealing with homesickness

Research on homesickness shows that it comes from our need to belong, which is a basic need for all of us. Students who feel accepted by their new community are less likely to be homesick, so it is the community's attitude towards the newcomer that is important. For this reason, it is necessary to find people who are very welcoming towards you if you are an international student. There are support people attached to educational institutions that will help you feel welcome, and someone may even have the specific job of being your support person. It is also very helpful to make Australian friends.

The more homesick you are, the more likely it is that you will call or email home frequently. Researchers have also found that talking on the phone to your friends and family overseas doesn't decrease homesickness, but that it is a comfort. The good news is that there is also evidence to suggest that the more you involve yourself with your temporary life in Australia, the less you will need to make contact with people at home.

Typical pressures on international students

As you will have seen from the previous case studies, international students face additional pressures to Australian students. These pressures are often very real, such as those resulting from financial or language issues. The following is an exercise to help you think about the extra pressures you face as an international student.

Exercise 46: identifying the pressures you face as an international student

Below is a list of typical pressures experienced by international students. These difficulties tend to increase if you come from a culture that is very different to your host country's, but the good news is that they tend to decrease the longer you stay. Read the list and then put a tick next to the statements that sound familiar to you. If you are a 'typical' international student you will probably find yourself ticking quite a few. If you want to add any other pressures you are feeling write them in your notebook. The point of this exercise is to remember that it is normal to feel this way.

- ☐ My visa requirements mean I must keep making academic progress.
- ☐ I want to finish my course as soon as possible because I am privately funded — the longer I stay the more expensive my education is.
- ☐ The university systems, technology, method of teaching and communication styles are all very different to those back home.
- ☐ My language difficulties slow down my reading, writing and verbal communication.
- ☐ My language difficulties may not be taken into account when my exams are marked.
- ☐ I don't like eating unfamiliar food.
- ☐ I have difficulty living in unfamiliar weather patterns.
- ☐ I find it hard to ask for help.
- ☐ I am afraid of 'losing face' if I return home without qualifying or if I have not done well enough.
- ☐ I am homesick.
- ☐ My family and friends at home don't understand the difficulties I am facing.

☐ My language difficulties mean I work slower than my Australian peers, so I think I'm not performing as well as they are.

☐ I am afraid of 'losing face' or being seen as having a mental illness if I ask for help from a counsellor.

Although this list sounds horrible, staff in educational institutions usually understand the problems faced by international students and will do their best to help you through these difficulties. You must ask for help if you need it.

Adjustment takes time

I mentioned earlier that problems and issues seem to resolve themselves the longer an international student remains in their host country. Adjusting to any new culture or lifestyle change takes time. Have a look at figure 13.1.

Figure 13.1: curve of adjustment — coming to your host country to study

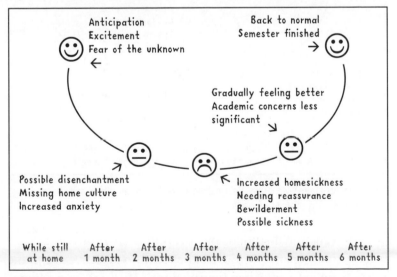

This curve shows that an international student normally feels initial anticipation and excitement at the prospect of going overseas to study, and that this feeling normally lasts until the student reaches their host country and reality sets in. There is then a period of feeling grief, frustration and anxiety, as the student is still getting used to their host country, the workings of the educational institution and a foreign language. Finally, the student 'finds their feet' and starts to feel more settled and less homesick. By this stage they have come up the other side of the curve. This whole process usually takes about six months, which for a university or college student is usually the whole of their first semester.

Now take a look at the curve in figure 13.2.

Figure 13.2: curve of adjustment — going home

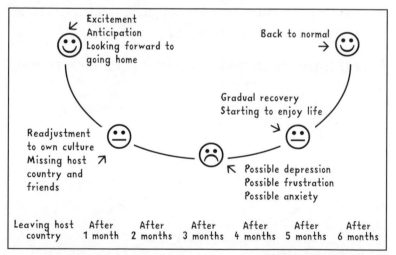

Source: adapted from Vivien Hope, University of Adelaide and Kay Clifford and Charlene Schmult, University of Michigan, 1989.

If an international student has been in their host country for a long time, chances are that they will experience the same curve of adjustment when they go home. When the time comes for you to leave your host country you will probably feel a sense of excitement about going home, but once the reality of being home sets in you may well find yourself missing the new friends you made in your host country, as well as its culture. As time passes, you will adjust to your own culture, family and friends again.

Patterns, script systems and the international student

Even though you will probably be feeling the pressures of visa requirements, homesickness, language problems and other 'normal' pressures of being an international student, you will probably also be feeling pressure from your own set of cultural values. Your borrowed and child patterns and the contents of your script may be quite different from typical Australian ones. You may have been brought up to not let anyone know if you have a problem, and so for this reason you may feel ashamed about asking for help. Perhaps you come from a culture where you would be ashamed if you got low marks. Having such messages in your patterns and script is not helpful when you are studying within the Australian culture, and would also cause problems if you were studying back home.

It is not possible to cover all cultures here; however, when you did the exercises in the previous chapters you would have been thinking about your own child and borrowed patterns and your script, and these would have reflected your own culture. It may have been hard to challenge your thoughts and behaviours, but the exercises and hints can go a long way towards helping you cope with these extra pressures. If challenging your thoughts is particularly difficult for you then perhaps it would be useful to ask yourself how you might advise a friend from your own culture in the same situation.

Extra hints for international students

In addition to the previous, here are some extra hints specifically written for international students.

⇨ Pay particular attention to challenging the thoughts that are making you anxious. Remind yourself of the thoughts you challenged in chapter 6, and how you dealt with memories and fantasies in chapter 7.

⇨ Make sure that you ask for help when you need it. This may be academic help, administrative help, help from your friends, or help from a counsellor. Remember that staff in educational institutions understand that you may need some extra assistance and are generally willing to give it.

⇨ Remember that using the support networks at your educational institution will probably decrease any homesickness you may be experiencing.

⇨ Watch the internal bodily experiences in your script system. If you see or feel any warning signs then make sure you follow the hints that I gave you, particularly those in chapter 4.

⇨ Pay particular attention to dealing with problems with perfection, as explained in chapter 8.

⇨ If English is not your first language, make sure you give yourself extra time for revision.

⇨ If you are experiencing so much homesickness that you find it hard to study, pay particular attention to the ideas on revising while coping with a large crisis or event, as explained in chapter 5. When studying, put photos of your loved ones back home out of sight so you can concentrate more easily.

⇨ Remember that students from your host country will probably write faster than you in the exam room, but it is quality, not quantity, that counts when marking exam papers. Most subjects are marked on the content of exam answers rather than style.

⇨ Different cultures offer different means of staying calm. In many cultures meditation and prayer help calm an anxious person. Use methods from your own culture to keep your body in a calm and relaxed state.

⇨ Don't be ashamed to use the counselling service at your institution. Counselling is for students who are psychologically healthy, but who are facing particular difficulties they would like some help to solve.

Exercise 47: final reminders for international students

Now that you have read this chapter for international students, I'd like to finish up by asking you to complete the sentences below in your notebook. They will act as a reminder whenever you are beginning to feel anxious.

⇨ When I begin to make myself anxious with my thoughts I will think about … instead.

⇨ When I see or feel any bodily signs of anxiety I will …

Enjoy your time in Australia!

Chapter summary

In this chapter you learned that:

⇨ international students are under additional pressures that can cause anxiety, and it is normal to feel these pressures

⇨ being welcomed by your host community decreases your homesickness

⇨ adjustment to a new culture takes time

⇨ when you eventually go home you may initially have trouble adjusting to your home culture

⇨ your patterns and script system stem from your own culture and these may cause problems in Australia

⇨ it is helpful to ask yourself how you would advise a friend from your own culture who has the same problems.

In addition, you:

⇨ identified the extra pressures of being an international student

⇨ were given extra hints on how to cope.

Chapter 14

Special hints for students who have migrated to Australia or who come from migrant families

This chapter is for those students who have migrated to Australia, and also for those who were born in Australia to migrant parents and where the influence of their parents' culture is still very strong. In other words, this chapter is for students who are under the influence of two different cultures.

If you can relate to this chapter it will probably also be useful for you to read the previous chapter for international students, as these students are also exposed to two cultures. The difference is that international students know they are eventually going home, while for migrant students their new country is their home. Both groups of students have to go through the curve of adjustment described in chapter 13, but international students have to repeat the process when they eventually get home after finishing their studies.

If you have only been in Australia for a short time you may be experiencing some of the same issues faced by international students, such as language, food and climate problems. You may also be feeling homesick, and your homesickness may be worsened by the knowledge that you will not actually be going 'home' in the near future.

If you have been in Australia for a while, or were perhaps even born here, you may feel resistant to reading this chapter because you don't feel these issues relate to you. However, some people born into a migrant family don't see their own culture as the same as their parents' culture, and this realisation can lead to an identity crisis, particularly if their peers still see them as 'different'. Experience shows that having the influence of patterns and scripts from two — often conflicting — cultures can be hard, although having a foot in two cultures can also be a rewarding experience. There are hints in this chapter to help you make it easier on yourself.

Migrants who enrol in some sort of study in their new country of residence experience various difficulties, depending on the culture they have come from. As you can imagine, students migrating from New Zealand and the United Kingdom probably have less difficulty adjusting to Australia's educational system than those coming from countries such as China or India, and therefore they will experience less anxiety in this respect. But they can still face difficulties that can be stressful.

Here are four case studies that illustrate the difficulties students from migrant families can face.

Adhira

Adhira was born in Australia—her parents migrated from India to Australia two years before she was born. Her brother was born in India and was only a baby when he arrived in Australia. The whole family has Australian citizenship.

Adhira's parents have high expectations of her. They expect her to do well academically and to marry into a suitable Indian family, to a well-educated husband. For this reason, they spent a great deal of money on private school fees, and Adhira is now studying law. Her parents are hoping she finds a suitable husband at university.

Adhira, though, is very Australian. She sounds Australian, has an Australian social network and has no interest in marrying into an Indian family. In fact, she has no interest in or aptitude for law, but enrolled to keep her parents happy, and has been spending more time partying than studying.

When exams come upon her quite suddenly, Adhira realises she has not left herself enough time to study for them. Panic sets in and she goes to the counselling service hoping to find some sort of magic solution that will enable her to pass, and to pass well enough to keep her parents happy. There is no time to deal with the cause of her anxiety, so the counsellor gives her some bandaid hints and offers to see her after the exams to help her deal with the problems causing her anxiety.

Adhira *(cont'd)*

Adhira is caught between two cultures. Her parents want her to marry into a suitable Indian family and Adhira does not want this, but she carries the borrowed pattern of 'children should do what their parents say' and her child wish is to keep them happy.

The case of Shen illustrates another cultural difficulty that can make some migrant students very anxious about their exams.

Shen

Shen immigrated to Australia from China with his parents when he was 14. He learned English at school and picked up the language well enough to do reasonably well. His parents have still not learned English, preferring to stay within the Chinese community and rely on him to translate for them when necessary. Their reliance on their son is more than just for language—they expect him to go to university, get a high-paying job and support them financially. Shen is aware of their expectations and thinks that it is his duty to support them once he has graduated. For this reason, the stakes are high for Shen.

Shen studies for many hours in the lead-up to exams, giving himself very little time for leisure and pleasure.

He makes himself extremely anxious and becomes ill with a skin disease as a consequence. The doctor tells Shen that he needs to take the rest of the semester off to recover. By the time the counsellor gets to see him, Shen is feeling very depressed about letting his parents down. The counsellor helps him deal with his exam anxiety and associated problems so that when it is time for Shen to re-enrol he can do so without anxiety.

Alice, like Adhira earlier, was born in Australia to migrant parents. Alice's heritage is Vietnamese and her case study illustrates how she is caught between the two cultures of Vietnam and Australia, and how this conflict increases her exam anxiety.

Alice

Alice lives on the opposite side of the city to her university. It takes her well over an hour to travel each way, and the busses are so crowded that she finds it too hard to concentrate on reading while travelling. Vietnamese cultural values include that a child should not move out of home until they get married, that girls should not have a boyfriend until they finish studying, and that when they do he should be Asian (preferably Vietnamese). Alice's parents tell her repeatedly that they sacrificed a lot to come to Australia so that their children could have a better life than they did.

Alice *(cont'd)*

Alice wants to move out of home to live with a group of friends she made at university (but her parents said no), and she is tired of keeping her boyfriend a secret. She is also tired of all the travelling and wants to use these hours for study in the library. Her exams are getting closer and she is worried that she is behind in her revision schedule. As Alice's exam anxiety increases, so does the conflict with her parents. Without the pressure of exams she can cope with the cultural differences between them, but by the time she seeks help at the counselling service her exam anxiety is high and life at home is becoming unbearable.

Through counselling Alice decides to be more accepting of her parent's values, realising they are not likely to change. This decision helps her manage her stress level, and therefore her exam anxiety. She also decides that she will enlist the help of a Vietnamese counselling service over the summer break, with the hope that her parents will also attend and perhaps soften their app-roach regarding Alice's needs and desires. By deciding to be more relaxed about her parents' values, at least for a while, she is able to focus on her exams with just the right amount of pressure to do her best and stay at the top of the curve described in chapter 1.

Simon's case study illustrates that it is not only cultural differences that contribute to exam anxiety; the yearning for 'home' can also make students feel depressed and anxious.

Simon

Simon's parents migrated from England to Australia in time for Simon's last two years of high school. His older brother had just finished school in the United Kingdom, so it seemed a good time to make the move, as they had been planning it for some time. Once in Australia Simon's brother found himself an apprenticeship and Simon finished his schooling. When it was time for Simon to move on to tertiary study his brother decided to go back to England. He was missing his friends and hadn't been able to adjust well to living in Australia. Simon was devastated when his brother moved back, and regular contact with his brother by email and webcam made him think long and hard about which country he wanted to live in. He was so preoccupied with trying to decide that he found it hard to get on with studying for his exams. The closer the exams came, the more anxious he became.

Simon asked for help and a counsellor introduced him to the 'time out for worry' technique that was explained in chapter 5. Using this technique Simon was able to study for his exams (and pass). Part of his 'time out for worry' was spent talking with the counsellor, and during these sessions Simon decided to stay in Australia until he finished his degree. He would decide later what would happen after that. Once he knew for sure that he was going to stay in the country and finish his degree Simon settled back into his university life very well.

These four case studies illustrate some typical pressures that migrant students face. Some pressures, such as Shen's pressure to do well and get a good job, are directly related to results; other pressures, such as Alice not being allowed to leave home, are not directly related to results, but add to the pressure students face, toppling them over the top of the curve described in chapter 1.

What are the pressures on you as a migrant? The exercise below will help you work this out.

Exercise 48: identifying the pressures you face as a migrant

As with international students, the difficulties faced by migrant students tend to increase if your family is from a very different culture to the one you have settled in, but the longer you are in your 'new' country, the easier it becomes. Even if the two cultures are fairly similar, it still takes time to adjust. To give you a personal example, I migrated from England to Australia without my family as an adult. I had been here for about seven years when I found myself cheering the Australian cricket team rather than the English team in a test match. When I realised what I was doing I also realised I was 'home'!

Below is a list of the typical pressures faced by migrant students. Read the list and then put a tick next to those that feel familiar to you. If you want to add any other pressures you are feeling write them in your notebook.

☐ My values are different from my parents' cultural values and this is difficult for me.

☐ I am expected to support my parents by helping them financially, culturally and linguistically.

☐ I am homesick for my 'old' country and my friends or relatives who live there.

☐ I feel pressure from my family to go to university because they never did and want me to be the first in the family to do so.

☐ I feel pressure from my family to succeed.

☐ I am enrolled in a course that doesn't suit my interests or abilities because it is what my parents want me to do.

☐ I am struggling with gaps in my previous education because of my move.

☐ I am experiencing poverty.

☐ My language skills are less developed and are making study more difficult.

The good news!

Assessing the pressures on you as a migrant student, whether you were born here or not, can be negative if you do not also assess the positives of your or your family's move to a new country. An example of a positive experience might be that you have the widened experience of knowing about two cultures and can probably feel comfortable in either of them. Your life experiences are also more than likely greater than those of fellow students who have only ever experienced one culture.

Exercise 49: recognising the positives of being a migrant student

In your notebook write down the positive aspects of being born into a migrant family or being a migrant yourself.

Patterns, script systems and the migrant student

Whether you were born here or not, you will still have your own borrowed and child patterns and your own script system that can make you anxious over exams, just like any other exam-anxious student. As I explained in the chapter on international students, our patterns and script systems are very closely linked to our culture, so it is not possible for me to give examples that would suit all migrant students. Using the case studies provided in this chapter, Adhira seems to be operating with the borrowed pattern of 'I must do what my parents say', but her child patterns are rebellious. Shen seems to be operating from the belief that 'it is right to financially support your parents', but his internal bodily experience is a cry for adult insight to take control. Alice seems to have a borrowed pattern of 'I must obey my parents', but her adult insight allows her to be relaxed about it and make plans to deal with it after exams. For Simon the need to obey his parents does not seem to be an issue, at least on the surface, but he could be influenced by a belief that brothers should stick together.

When you did the exercises earlier in this book you would have been thinking about your own child and borrowed patterns and your script system, and these may have reflected your 'old' culture, even if you were born in Australia. By completing all the previous exercises and following the corresponding hints, you too can manage your anxiety so that it doesn't interfere

with your performance in exams, because the exercises and
hints in this book apply to all cultures.

Extra hints for migrant students

The hints given for international students in the previous
chapter will also be relevant to you. Below is a list of additional
hints for migrant students.

⇨ Work hard at dealing with issues in your patterns and
script system that are tied up with unhelpful aspects
of your 'old' culture you want to change.

⇨ Take pride in belonging to two cultures and use your
adult insight to integrate the best aspects of both.
For example, use methods of relaxation that work for
you, regardless of which culture they reflect.

⇨ Communicate with your parents about the differences
between their culture and your new culture,
particularly in the area of study. You may need to
enlist the help of others who know your old culture
well and perhaps speak the language.

⇨ Make sure you are enrolled in a course that *you* want
to do, not a course that your parents want you to do.

⇨ Make sure you seek out friendships with Australians,
as well as with people from your 'old' country.

Exercise 50: final reminders for migrant students

Now that you have read this chapter specifically for migrant
students, I'd like to end by asking you to complete the
following sentences in your notebook.

⇨ The borrowed patterns that my adult insight needs to watch out for are ...

⇨ The child patterns that my adult insight needs to watch out for are ...

⇨ When I begin to make myself anxious with my thoughts I will think about ... instead.

⇨ When I see or feel bodily signs of anxiety I will ...

Enjoy the richness of living with two cultural influences.

Chapter summary

In this chapter you learned that:

⇨ you can experience the difficulties of living with two cultural influences even if you were born in Australia

⇨ living with two cultural influences has many advantages

⇨ some of the pressures you experience are directly related to exams, while others are more to do with your cultural lifestyle, which can cause anxiety, too.

In addition, you:

⇨ identified the pressures you face as a migrant, or the child of a migrant family

⇨ identified the positives of living within two cultures

⇨ were given extra hints for migrant students

⇨ made promises to yourself that will remind you to control your anxiety.

Part VI

My exams have arrived!

The world is round and the place which may seem like the end may also be the beginning.

— Ivy Baker Priest

If you have now read the beginning of this book and listened to the CD, you will know what drives your exam anxiety and you have hopefully brought your pressure level under control so that you can perform at your personal best. You are probably on your way to ridding yourself of any perfectionist and procrastination tendencies you may have had, and if you fall into one of the groups of students in part V, you have hopefully started to deal with any special issues and concerns you may have.

This part has only one chapter, which includes advice on what to do in the evening before a morning exam, what to do in the morning before an afternoon exam, and what to do when you are in the exam room to remain calm and focused.

It's also time to see how much this book has helped you overcome your anxiety to take your exams with no worries.

Chapter 15

Final advice

Now that your exams are almost here, it's time to have a look at how you can prepare yourself when they actually arrive.

What to do ...

In the evening before a morning exam

You don't have to do any more revision at this point, but I know that some students can't help themselves! Whatever you do, don't try to learn anything new at this point. Only do minor revision tasks such as going over your notes.

What to do ... *(cont'd)*

- If you have to revise, don't revise right up until bedtime. Do something relaxing, such as listening to music or taking a bath, before you go to bed.

- If you are going to be taking an oral exam, rehearse your entry into the exam room and your answers out loud, keeping your centering breath flowing calmly.

- Take lots of breaks between tasks and do something 'real', such as watching the news or phoning a friend. Remind yourself of how your exam fits into the wider context of your life, as it really is only a small part of your life as a whole.

- Don't drink alcohol or take any non-prescription drugs. You need an uninterrupted sleep so you can wake up clear-headed.

- Don't eat or drink anything you know will upset your digestive system (some students find that their digestive system tends to mirror the amount of pressure they are experiencing).

- Get your clothes ready for the next day. If you have a choice, wear something loose and comfortable that makes you feel good. Layer your clothes so you can adjust to the temperature of the exam room.

- Have a reasonably early night. Follow the instructions in chapter 4 for getting a good night's sleep, or fall asleep listening to the last track on the CD if that helps.

- Never take a sleeping pill the night before an exam. Not only can you wake up feeling groggy, you may wake up late for the exam!

- Don't revise early the next morning. If you do, your energy for the exam may decrease and it can also muddle your thinking.

- Plan to arrive at the exam room the next morning so you only have about 15 minutes to wait before you go in. This way you can steer clear of anxious people fairly easily.

In the morning before an afternoon exam

- Try to keep your morning free of stressful events. For example, do your best to avoid paid employment, or at least give yourself a big break before going to the exam. The same goes for looking after your children or any other activity that can leave you feeling stressed.

- Make sure you had an early night. Follow the instructions in chapter 4 for getting a good night's sleep, or fall asleep listening to the last track on the CD.

- Do some gentle exercise to keep your energy level up and practise your centering.

- If you must revise, don't try to learn anything new, but rather do smaller tasks. Take lots of breaks between these tasks and give yourself a good break from revision before the exam.

- Stay real about your exam and see it in perspective. After all, it is only a small part of your life.

What to do ... *(cont'd)*

- Avoid coffee if you tend to get 'caffeine shakes'.

- Don't eat or drink anything just before the exam, so you can be sure you won't have to make a mad dash to the bathroom during the exam.

- If you have a choice, wear something loose and comfortable that makes you feel good. Layer your clothes so you can adjust to the temperature of the exam room.

- Plan to arrive at the exam room so you only have about 15 minutes to wait before you go in. This way you can steer clear of anxious people fairly easily.

In the exam room

By now you will know how to stay calm and focused, but there are a few more hints I can give you that are specific to being in the exam room. Remember, I am only going to tell you things to help you stay calm — I am not going to tell you how to write a good exam answer. There are plenty of study skills books that tell you how to do this, and some are mentioned in the further reading list at the end of the book. You will have already imagined doing some of the hints described below when you listened to track 3 on the CD.

- Start your exam with a plan for your time distribution during the exam. If you can write on your question paper in your reading time, write out your timing of the exam. Pace yourself to start each question at the time you have written down because spending more time on one question and therefore less time on another can lose you marks.

- Read the question paper slowly and carefully. If you misread a question you may panic.

- Start with the question you feel most confident about if you want to boost your confidence. If one question is worth more marks you may want to start with that one, as energy levels are usually higher at the start of an exam.

- If you get stuck on an essay-type question, rather than allowing yourself to get anxious, think about any summaries you have written on the topic, as these will help jog your memory.

- If you get stuck on a multiple-choice answer, leave it and go on to the next, returning to it at the end of the exam. Research shows that when students change answers on a multiple-choice paper they change wrong answers to right answers about twice as often as they change right answers to wrong answers.

- If you get stuck on a calculation-type question, use the technique suggested by your teacher when you asked for information on the exam.

- If you have a memory lapse, leave a gap and continue on with the question if possible. We often remember when we are not trying to. If this happens, you can go back and fill in the gaps.

What to do ... *(cont'd)*

- Remember to take a few centering breaths from time to time, particularly between questions. This helps you clear your mind of the last question before going on to the next.

- If you are taking an oral exam, centre yourself while waiting outside the exam room. Remember that the exam starts as soon as you walk in, so do whatever is appropriate (such as introducing yourself) with confidence. Use your posture, eye contact and smile to boost your confidence.

- Remember that there is no reward for finishing first. Use all your time according to the timing you have set for yourself.

- If your pacing goes wrong and you do run out of time, write rough notes for the last question and include a note to the marker about why your answer is in note form. Getting something down for your last answer will probably bring you more marks than simply adding to previous answers.

- Don't forget to give yourself a reward once the exam is over!

You have now reached the end of your journey into discovering the causes of your exam anxiety and learning how to overcome them. To consolidate your learning, take some time now to think back over the book and CD package. You have been on a long journey.

Exercise 51: summing up what you have learned from this book

Imagine you have a close friend who is anxious about exams. They know you have worked your way through this book and CD and ask you what you got out of doing so. After all, it's been a long process. What do you tell them? (Write your answers in your notebook.)

Now choose three ideas or techniques that really stood out for you and tell your anxious friend, 'Whatever you do, make sure you ...'

There is one last exercise for you to do once your exam (or exams) is over. Do the following, and last, exercise after having taken one or more exams since reading this book.

Exercise 52: finding out if this book worked for you

Look back to how you rated your exam anxiety in the preface of this book. Here is the same chart again in table 15.1 (overleaf), this time with two more columns for your responses now that you have read the book and taken an exam. Transfer your old ratings to the first two columns, and then put your new ratings in the last two columns.

Remember not to confuse necessary pressure with anxiety. We all need some pressure to do our personal best, but it is only when we have too much that we become anxious.

Table 15.1: my anxiety rating before and after reading the book

	Before		After	
My anxiety level	When exams are close	During an exam	When exams are close	During an exam
I have no anxiety	0	0	0	0
I am slightly anxious	1	1	1	1
I am fairly anxious	2	2	2	2
I am very anxious	3	3	3	3
I am extremely anxious	4	4	4	4
I am in a total panic	5	5	5	5

Congratulations! Take good exams and take care.

Su Dorland.

Chapter summary

In this chapter you learned:

⇨ what to do in the evening before a morning exam

⇨ what to do in the morning before an afternoon exam

⇨ what to do in the exam room to stay calm and focused

In addition, you identified:

⇨ what you got out of the book and CD
⇨ what stood out for you in terms of hints and techniques.

Finally, after you had taken one or more exams you:

⇨ rated your current level of anxiety over exams and compared it to your rating when you first picked up the book.

Further reading

If you are interested in reading more about topics covered in this book, the following titles may be useful. The list is not exhaustive. All the books and articles are available in Australia.

Taking exams

Orr, F 2004, *How to Pass Exams*, Allen & Unwin, Australia.
This (as the title suggests) is a book about how to pass exams. Only a small section is devoted to dealing with exam anxiety.

General study skills

Carr-Gregg, M 2004, *Surviving Year 12*, Finch, Australia.
This is a general book written for final-year school children and their parents.

Grellier, J & Goerke, V 2006, *Communication Skills Toolkit: Unlocking the Secrets of Tertiary Success*, Thomson Social Science Press, Australia.
This book is about written and oral communication for tertiary students.

Marshall, L & Rowland, F 2006, *A Guide to Learning Independently*, 4th edn, Pearson Longman, Australia.
This is a particularly useful book for mature-age and off-campus students.

Rose, C 1985, *Accelerated Learning*, 5th edn, Accelerated Learning Systems Ltd, UK.

This popular book has gone through many editions and is good for help with concentration and memory.

Turner, K, Ireland, L, Krenus, B & Pointon, L 2008, *Essential Academic Skills*, Oxford University Press, Australia.

This is a general academic skills book for university students.

Anxiety

Bourne, E 2005 *The Anxiety and Phobia Workbook*, New Harbinger, USA.

This book is full of exercises to help rid you of anxiety.

Bourne, E & Garano, L 2003, *Coping with Anxiety*, New Harbinger, USA.

This is a useful guide for coping with anxiety.

Foreman, E, Elliott, C & Smith, L 2007, *Overcoming Anxiety for Dummies*, John Wiley & Sons, UK.

This is an easy-to-read guide for dealing with anxiety.

Cognitive behaviour therapy

Willson, R & Branch, R 2006, *Cognitive Behaviour Therapy for Dummies*, John Wiley & Sons, UK.

This is an easy-to-understand guide to cognitive behaviour therapy.

Transactional analysis

Lapworth, P, Sills, C & Fish, S 1993, *Transactional Analysis Counselling*, Winslow Press, UK.

Stewart, I & Joines, V 1987, *T A Today: A New Introduction to Transactional Analysis*, Lifespace Publishing, UK.
Both these books are currently used by students of TA and are considered excellent basic books on the subject. Both contain self-help exercises and ideas.

Articles referred to in the text

Erskine, R & Zalcman, M 1979, 'The Racket System: a model for racket analysis', *Transactional Analysis Journal*, vol. 9, no.1, pp. 293–301.
I have adapted the concept of script systems (first mentioned in part I) from the racket system devised by Erskine and Zalcman.

Rendon, L 1998, cited in O'Shea, S 2007, 'Well, I got here… but what happens next?', *Journal of the Australia and New Zealand Student Services Association*, no. 29, April, pp. 36–51.
This article was referred to in part V and cites research on mature-age students.

Watt, SE & Badger, AJ 2009, 'Effects of social belonging on homesickness: An application of the belongingness hypothesis', *Personality and Social Psychology Bulletin*, vol. 35, p. 516.
This article was referred to in part V and cites research on international students and homesickness.

Index